# GREAT FOOD FOR GREAT KIDS

Quick & Easy Recipes for a Healthy Family

by MEYERA ROBBINS

Published by Michael Wiese Productions, 4354 Laurel Canyon Blvd., Suite 234, Studio City, CA 91604 for Great Kids Partners, (818) 379-8799

Cover design by Chris Whorf, Art Hotel, Los Angeles
Cover Photo from American Stock Photography

Printed by Braun-Brumfield, Inc., Ann Arbor, Michigan
Manufactured in the United States of America

Printed on Recycled Paper
ISBN 0-9639992-0-6


Robbins, Meyera.
      Great food for great kids : quick and easy recipes for a healthy family / by Meyera Robbins.
      p.   cm.
      ISBN 0-9639992-0-6
      1. Vegetarian cookery. 2. Quick and easy cookery. I. Title.
TX837.R57      1994
641.5 '636--dc20                              94-13524
                                                 CIP

# TABLE OF CONTENTS

# CONTENTS

## SANDWICHES AND LUNCH

## SPREAD & DIPS

## STOCKS, SOUPS, GRAVIES & SAUCES

## SALADS

# BIOGRAPHY

I started cooking interesting foods while living in New York City, where a group of my friends would assemble on Saturday nights to enjoy each other's company and dine together. Experimenting just became a natural process, and so I found myself cooking exotic and unfamiliar foods for 20 to 30 people at a time. I worked in several restaurants in Manhattan and after moving to Los Angeles, I opened my own restaurant in Santa Monica called Meyera. The menu at Meyera was strictly lacto-ovo-vegetarian (vegetarian with dairy and egg dishes), and we had many non-dairy items on the menu. As the years passed and after the restaurant sold, I began to cook purely for us at home. We eat very little dairy. In fact, my daughter's cholesterol is 108. I sometimes cater parties and am always careful to serve clean, ungreasy, fresh foods.

I was born in Philadelphia and raised on meat and potato dinners. We had a chicken night and a dairy night, etc. It took a lot of mind-bending to begin to change. Through the years, although health is the primary concern, the taking of an animal's life for food just began to seem repulsive. It's also so wasteful to feed cows the grain that could directly go on our tables.

I'm sure many people think Jay and I are radical in our beliefs, but I have trouble sleeping if I am wasteful of our resources or especially if I eat poorly. I hope my recipes and ideas will be helpful to you.

Good Luck!!

# ACKNOWLEDGMENTS

I'd like to thank a few of my friends who, over the years, have inspired me to create through cooking. Ruth Kurtzman, who taught me to experiment and enjoy my mistakes. Kathleen Burke and David Spain who worked with me to interpret and adapt recipes for my restaurant.

Michael Wiese has been the only person in my life who has been able to make me write down my recipes. Ken Lee and Robin Quinn for their tireless energy in editing this book from my longhand copies because I don't know how to type or use a computer.

To Simone, my daughter, who always asks me to prepare her early dinner while I'm preparing our meal ...and then eats again with us. Simone has taught me that kids can and will eat healthy foods readily and are proud of it.

And finally, to my wonderful husband who is more than just an inspiration, but also a taster for my ideas and very true to his health and moral principles. He keeps me honest in our vegetarian concepts.

# INTRODUCTION

# INTRODUCTION

If you are reading this book, you are probably concerned about your health, as well as the health of your family and of the planet. What we eat relates directly to how we care about ourselves and the world in which we live. Contributing to the future health of the planet is a passionate, time-consuming interest of mine.

Years ago when I started to become aware of environmental issues my focus was on the problem of littering. My interest in litter led to a concern about packaging. At the same time my love for animals directed me toward the road to a vegetarian diet. At the time I was unaware of the incredible waste which was involved with eating animals. In "Diet for a New America" by John Robbins, the facts are stated. Acquaint yourself with this insightful book. Robbins points out that it takes many more pounds of plant food to feed animals than the yield is worth.

Well, one thing led to another. I love to eat and especially to dine. By nature I enjoy creating, so the natural progression was to cook enjoyable tasty foods.

The recipes in this book are all vegetarian. If this way of eating is new to you, don't try to eliminate all meats immediately. Find out what you and your family enjoy and steadily increase the portions of vegetables and fruits while you decrease the portions of meat.

1

Change your pantry and refrigerator products to reflect health consciousness. Try to stay away from canned and heavily packaged food. Reuse plastic bags; recycle constantly. Compost, if you can. Start a garden; even a window garden for herbs and lettuce can be incredibly rewarding. Always ask for organic produce in the markets. The more that people ask for organic goods the sooner the demand will be met. Shop at the health food store before you go to the market. Buy new products and try them.

Buy bio-degradable products. Eliminate most of your paper towels and napkins by using cloth napkins and dish towels.

Try to experiment with different ingredients, remembering that there really aren't any failures. As you change your expectations about the types of food you prepare, you're bound to become a satisfied cook! Buy a wok! You will love it! It is so easy to use and to clean. You never know what you and your family will enjoy until you try it! Start now. There is no better time.

# TIPS & HINTS

# TIPS & HINTS

Without customers, supermarkets and country stores would not exist. And although there are always some uncaring, uncooperative companies, I have found it's pretty easy to get what you want if you ask for it. So here are some shopping, eating, cooking, and living ideas.

1. Always ask for organic produce and fruit.

2. Ask for grains, juices, and exotic foods that you do not find available. All big distributors carry a huge selection of goods that are just waiting to be shipped out.

3. Buy seasonal, local fresh foods. This is a good way to introduce yourself to produce that you have never tried before. It's also a good way to feel the seasons change and be a part of the earth.

4. Wash all produce, even organic. You never know how it has been handled.

5. Make sprouts. It's fun for the kids and it's wonderfully healthy. When you sprout beans, seeds, and legumes, their fat content decreases while the amounts of vitamin B & C that they contain increase!

6. Make double batches of soups, beans, and sauces, and freeze or use them as leftovers. It's nice to have a day off from cooking!

7.    Keep a lot of fresh fruits on hand.

8.    Keep a dip or two and cut up vegetables in the refrigerator for snacking.

9.    Remember, it may be necessary to introduce new foods several times and in different ways before they are accepted by your family.

10.    Proceed slowly. Introduce snacks, desserts, and side dishes first. A side dish or appetizer can later become a main course.

11.    Eat only when hungry. Allow snacking of 'good' food no matter when. This will help prevent dietary problems in later life.

12.    Don't be discouraged. Sometimes my daughter only wants pastas and pancakes. Sometimes I feel exactly like that too!

13.    Remember, being healthy is more than the absence of sickness. It means being aware, alert, stimulated, and at one with the earth.

# HELPFUL DEFINITIONS

*Chop* - Cut up food; usually the size is specified.

*Cube* - Cut up food into a specific shape.

*Dice* - Smaller cubes.

*Diagonal Cut* - To cut on an angle; known as "macrobiotic cut".

*Julienne* - Food cut into long thin strips, size usually specified.

*Liquefy* - To process ingredients into a blender to liquid state.

*Mince* - Food chopped into tiny bits.

*Purée* - To liquefy ingredients; usually thicker than liquefying.

*Shred* - Food cut into long thin pieces.

*Slice* - Food cut into flat-sided pieces.

# SHOPPING LIST

# SHOPPING LIST

Keep as many of these produce products on hand as possible. Slowly eliminate junk foods and start shopping at the health food store before going to the market. Experiment with new products. Slowly eliminate all the high fat and junk food in your diet. You may find you don't have to go to the regular supermarket.

agar agar (like gelatin, but from seaweed)
apple butter
applesauce -
baking soda
baking powder without aluminum
beans - all kinds and colors
bran cereals
buckwheat flour
chips without oil
couscous
curry paste powder
Egg Beaters® or egg substitute
frozen corn
frozen cranberries
Gorilla Sauce® (barbecue sauce)
hot cereals
jams - organic
mung beans (for sprouting)

11

mustard, dry
mustard, prepared
no-egg noodles, etc.
organic corn flakes
organic pastas - macaroni, spaghetti
organic puffed rice, corn, and wheat
pita breads
Rice Dream®
sesame seeds
Smart Dogs® (soy hot dogs)
shredded wheat
sourdough rolls (no oil)
soy sauce
Wesbrae Soy Milk Lite or "Plus"(with calcium)
sunflower seeds
tortillas without lard
unbleached flours
unsulfured apricots
vegetable bouillon without salt
water bagels
water chestnuts
wheat germ
whole wheat bread and rolls
whole wheat flours

# FRESH FRUITS & VEGETABLES

Keep seasonal produce on hand, and learn how to prepare local foods in a healthy manner.

Apples
Asparagus
Avocados

Bananas
Berries
Broccoli
Cabbages
Carrots

Celery
Grapefruits
Herbs - fresh and dried
Jalapeno peppers

Leeks
Lemons
Lettuces

Mangoes
Melons
Onions - white, red, and green
Oranges
Papayas
Pears
Pineapples
Potatoes - try all kinds
Radishes
Salad greens
Garlic
Squash - acorn, butternut, summer, zucchini, yellow, spaghetti, and banana
Strawberries
Sweet potatoes

## COOKING GRAINS

Grains need not be pre-soaked before cooking.
Here is a chart to use as a cooking guide. For softer
grains, add a little more water or stock. For al dente
follow directions below.

| Grain (1 cup) | Grain/Water Cups | Cooking Time | Yield in Cups |
|---|---|---|---|
| Short Grain Brown Rice | 1 - 2 | 40 minutes covered/ let stand for 20 minutes covered | 3 |
| Barley | 1 - 2 1/2 | 40 minutes/ let stand for 10 minutes covered | 3 |
| Bulgar | 1 - 1 1/2 | 20 - 30 minutes | 2 1/2 |
| Couscous | 1 - 1 3/4 | 15 minutes | 1 1/2 |
| Buckwheat Oats | 1 - 2 | 20 - 30 minutes | 2 |
| Millet | 1 - 2 | 40 minutes | 3 1/4 |
| Basmati Rice | 1 - 2 | 20 minutes/ let stand for 10 minutes | 2 1/4 |
| Tritical | 1 - 3 | 1 1/2 hours/ let stand for 20 minutes | 2 1/2 |
| Taboule | 1 1/2 - 2 boiling | 20 minutes/ let stand for | 2 1/2 |
| Quinoa | 1 - 2 | 5 minutes 15 minutes / let stand for 10 minutes | 3 |

## COOKING BEANS

Most dried beans need to be soaked in water overnight or at least for 6 hours. Keep in a cool place. If it's a warm day or night, soak them in the refrigerator. Add a lot of water as they will soak up the liquid and sometimes double in size. Lentils do not need to be pre-soaked. Wash all beans first. Add plenty of water, and then soak.

The next day, drain water, and add fresh water, enough to cover the beans and then some. Simmer uncovered for at least 1 - 2 hours. Keep checking to make sure the water doesn't boil out. If you need to add some water, add boiling water.

1C of beans with 3C of water will yield approximately 2 1/2C cooked beans. If a recipe calls for cooked beans, you can used canned beans.

| Beans* | Water* | Cooking Time | Yield* |
|---|---|---|---|
| Aduki | 4 1/2 | 1 3/4 hrs. | 3 |
| Black Beans | 3 | 1 1/4 hrs. | 2 1/2 |
| Garbanzo | 6 1/2 | 3 1/2 hrs. | 3 |
| Kidney | 4 | 1 1/2 - 2 hrs. | 2 1/2 |
| Pinto | 5 | 1 1/2 - 2 hrs. | 2 1/2 |
| Red | 4 | 1 1/2 - 2 hrs. | 2 1/2 |
| Soy Beans | 6 | 3 | 2 1/2 |
| White | 5 | 2 | 2 1/2 |

* Measured as 1 cup.

16

# BREAKFAST
## How to Start The Day Right

## SWEET CREAM OF WHEAT

*Serves 2 to 3*

1/2C cream of wheat
1C water
2 tbs. chopped dates
1 tbs. golden raisins
dash of cinnamon
1/2C soy milk with vanilla

Bring water to a boil, and pour in the cream of wheat. Turn down heat and simmer. Stir in dried fruit and cinnamon. Remove from heat, and stir in soy milk.

NOTE: Sprinkling toasted wheat germ sprinkled on top creates a nice taste.

# RICE CREAM CEREAL

*Serves 4*

2C cooked short grain brown rice
1 1/2C soy milk plus with vanilla
1 tbs. honey
2 tbs. chopped dates
1/2 tbs. molasses
dash of nutmeg
dash of cinnamon

In a blender or food processor combine the following ingredients until smooth. (Divide ingredients in half, and repeat once if you are using the blender.) Heat gently and serve warm.

Bananas and strawberries may also be added.

## MILLET CEREAL

*Serves 4.*

1C millet
2C water
1 tbs. molasses
2 tbs. honey
1/3C shredded coconut
raisins or dates (optional)

In a blender, purée the millet to a fine grind. Bring water to a boil. Add the ground millet and stir. Turn down heat to simmer and add the fruit, molasses, and honey. Cook until soft and smooth, about 3 - 4 minutes.

Top with shredded coconut. If you want a thinner cereal, adding soy milk with vanilla tastes great!

## SOY PANCAKES

*Makes 8 pancakes.*

1/4C whole wheat flour
1/4C buckwheat flour
1/2C unbleached flour
1/2 tsp. baking powder (aluminum-free)

Combine dry ingredients in a bowl. Slowly add:
1C soy milk plus with vanilla.

Keep mixing, or blend in blender until smooth.
Sometimes I add an egg white, but I don't find it to be
essential.

Drop large spoonfuls onto a greased skillet.
When bubbles appear on top, flip it over for a few seconds and then transfer pancakes to a platter.

Serve with fresh fruit and fruit purées (see pureé
recipe in dessert section).

NOTE: To make crepes, use 1/8 - 1/4C more liquid.

For dinner crepes, use the soy milk <u>without</u>
vanilla and make sure they are <u>cool</u> before stacking
them (see recipe in Entrée Section).

For dessert crepes, use the soy milk with vanilla
for a sweeter taste.

# POTATO SQUASH PANCAKES

*Makes 10 to 12 pancakes.*

3 medium size potatoes
1 zucchini
1 sweet apple
1 onion
1/4 - 1/2C whole wheat flour

Shred the first four ingredients. Press out all the liquid by putting these ingredients in a strainer and pressing down with a spoon.

Transfer to a bowl, Add just enough of the whole wheat flour so the mixture stays together to form pancakes.

Use a non-stick griddle and make pancakes thin enough to cook well, but not too thin (or they will fall apart).

Brown them on one side and turn them over to brown the other side.

Tastes great with apple sauce.

# DRINKS

# BANANA & STRAWBERRY COMPOTE

1/2 c puréed strawberries
1/2 c orange juice
2 tbsp honey
1 cinnamon stick
dash of nutmeg
1 c of sliced fresh strawberries
1 c of sliced bananas
1/4 c raisins
1/2 c wheatgerm (optional)

Combine the first five ingredients, and heat until the honey is melted. Add the fruit and raisins, and simmer for 6 to 8 minutes. Serve warm with some chopped nuts or wheat germ sprinkled on top.

## MIXED FRUIT SMOOTHIES

In a blender, place:

1 c apple juice
1 banana
1 pear, diced (no need to peel it)
a dash of nutmeg

Blend until smooth, and pour into glasses.

*Variations:*

    *1) Start with apricot, pineapple, or orange juice.*

    *2) Blend in fresh strawberries.*

    *3) Add blueberries and grapes.*

    *4) Try orange juice with fresh pineapple and
       bananas.*

    *5) Mix soy milk with bananas or berries and a dash
       of vanilla.*

    *6) Add some honey (if the fruit isn't sweet enough).*

    *7) Freeze leftover smoothie mixture in a popsicle®
       mold with a stick handle, and serve as a treat.*

# STRAWBERRY SMOOTHIE

1C fresh washed strawberries
1 1/2 - 2C soy milk
1C crushed ice
1/2C fresh pear chopped (not necessary to peel)


    In a food processor, purée until smooth and thick. (This is the simplest and one of the tastiest early morning drinks. Any fresh fruit can be added or substituted.)

## PAPAYA SMOOTHIE

In a blender or food processor, combine:

1 papaya, peeled, seeded, and cubed
1C ice cubes or crushed ice
2 tbs. honey
juice of one lime
dash of vanilla

Blend until smooth. Soy milk can be added to thicken the drink. Just add 1/4 - 1/2C slowly.

## PINEAPPLE SMOOTHIE

In a blender or food processor, combine:

1C cubed pineapple chucks
1/2C soy milk with vanilla
1C ice cubes or crushed ice
1 tbs. lime juice

Blend until smooth and creamy.

# BANANA RICE SMOOTHIE

Blend until smooth:

1 small banana
2 chopped dates
1C soy milk plus with vanilla
1/4C cooked short grain brown rice

# ORANGE CRUSH DRINK

Blend until smooth:

1C orange juice
2 chopped dates
1 tsp. molasses or honey
1/4C soy milk with vanilla
1 tbs. protein powder
1C crushed ice

In season, any fresh berries can be added. If they are tart berries, add honey.

# PROTEIN ENERGY DRINK

1/4C sunflower seeds (softened)*
6 pitted large dates
2 1/2C orange juice

*Soak the seeds and dates in the juice for at least
    4 hours.

1/2C soy milk
1 tbs. vanilla
1 banana


Blend the softened seeds and dates with the
orange juice and the last 3 ingredients until
smooth. Add crushed ice.

NOTE: Apple or pineapple juice makes for a
good variation to this drink.

# GAZPACHO COCKTAIL

1 c chopped tomatoes
1 qrt tomato juice
1 tsp honey
dash of cumin
dash of coriander
1 tsp dry mustard
lemon juice
dash of hot pepper sauce
1 c carrots, chopped finely
1 c celery, chopped finely
1/4 c red onion minced
1 garlic clove, minced

Combine all ingredients in a blender, in 3 equal batches. It's not necessary to have a smooth purée. Some texture is tasty.

Garnish with fresh parsley and serve in chilled glasses.

# SANDWICHES
# & LUNCHES

# 4 PITA SANDWICH IDEAS

Pita bread is a thin bread with a pocket. Here are a variety of fillings:

**CALIFORNIAN:** Shredded lettuce, tomato slices, avocado slices, olives, alfalfa sprouts, grated soy cheese, and vinaigrette dressing.

**TOFU:** Marinated tofu cubes, chopped tomatoes, chopped avocado, shredded lettuce, toasted sesame seeds, red onion slices, and balsamic vinaigrette dressing.

**MEXICAN:** Refried beans, salsa, shredded lettuce, avocado slices, and, if available, fresh corn kernels and sprouts!

**FRENCH:** Mushrooms slices, shredded spinach, shredded soy cheese, grated carrots, chopped celery, mustard vinaigrette, and sunflower seeds.

# FRENCH OPEN FACED SANDWICH

Cut a 6" long French roll in half length-wise. Scoop out the white bread from both halves, and set aside. In a mixing bowl, combine all of the following ingredients and toss well.

1 tomato, chopped
1/2C chopped mushrooms
1C shredded spinach or arugola
1 tbs. chopped fresh parsley
1 tsp. chopped fresh basil
1/2C chopped cucumbers
3 tbs. balsamic vinegar
1/2C diced soy cheese (optional)

Fill the bottom half of the French roll with some of the vegetables, and close with the top half.

TIP: If you want a warm sandwich, toast the roll first and then fill it with vegetables and soy cheese. Broil the sandwich for a few short minutes, just enough to melt the cheese.

## "CAVIAR" ON TOAST

Toast thin bread slices and cut into triangles.

Spread Mushroom Caviar (see page 147) on each piece. Layer with chopped Belgium endive and finely minced red onion. Serve open face with sprinkles of parsley.

## "CAVIAR" HERO

In a French roll, layer:

Mushroom Caviar (See Recipe in Aside Section)
fresh mushroom slices
several baby greens
thinly sliced tomato
sunflower seeds

Sprinkle balsamic vinegar on the top half of the roll, and cover the sandwich. Enjoy!

# 4 ADDITIONAL IDEAS FOR COLD SANDWICHES

**WHOLE WHEAT BREAD** with green tahini spread (see page 58), tomatoes, lettuce, and cucumbers.

**BLACK BREAD WITH TOFU SPREAD** (see page 53), shredded carrots, and soy cheese slices.

**SOURDOUGH "HERO" ROLL** with green tahini spread, tomato slice and lots of sprouts.

**WHOLE WHEAT BREAD WITH GREEN GODDESS DRESSING**, (See Recipe in Salad Dressing Section) cucumbers, alfalfa sprouts, and marinated beans.

NOTES:

1. Try different sprouts. Radish sprouts tend to be tart and have a bite. Alfalfa, sunflower, and mung bean are milder. Mung bean sprouts are crunchy, and sunflower seed sprouts have a wonderful taste.

2. Keep toasted sesame seeds and chopped nuts handy.

3. When packing sandwiches for lunch boxes, use a piece of wax paper between the bread and wet ingredients to keep the bread from getting soggy. (Let it hang out so your child will see it and pull it out before biting into the sandwich).

# TOFU SLOPPY JOES

*Serves 4*

Prepare chili first.

1 onion, chopped
1/2C chopped celery
1/2C grated carrots
2 garlic cloves, minced
1 1/2C water
1C tomato sauce
1/4C diced green chilies
1/2 tsp. basil leaves
1/2 tsp. oregano leaves
1 tbs. chili powder
1 tsp. soy sauce
dash of Tabasco® (or more if you like it 'hot')
1C cooked kidney beans

Combine the first five ingredients in a saucepan. Simmer for 20 minutes, watching that the water doesn't boil out completely. Drain off any excess liquid, and add all the remaining ingredients.

Simmer for 30 minutes. Set aside.

*Continues...*

Prepare tofu:

1/2C water
1/2C soy sauce
1 tbs. balsamic vinegar
1 pound hard tofu, cut into small cubes

Combine first three ingredients. Add the tofu, and toss gently. Marinate for 10 minutes. Now take tofu cubes and spread them out on a cookie sheet.

Broil until brown, turning them over once or twice.

Add them to the chili mix. (You can save the marinade for a couple of weeks in a sealed jar in the refrigerator).

Fill "hero" rolls with chili-tofu mixture.

# MUSHROOM BURGER

*Makes 4 to 6 patties.*

1 - 2 tbs. safflower oil
1C chopped onions
2 garlic cloves, minced
1 1/2C chopped mushrooms
1C grated carrots
3/4C unsalted chopped peanuts
   (chop into a coarse meal)
1 tbs. curry powder
1 tbs. soy sauce
1/2 - 1C bread crumbs

Sauté the first three ingredients for 6 minutes and then add the mushrooms and carrots. Keep cooking for another 5 minutes. Pour the sauté into a mixing bowl and then add the next three ingredients.

Slowly add enough bread crumbs so that the mixture will form "burgers" easily. (It may be necessary to wash your hands clean periodically so that the mixture doesn't continue to stick to your hands). Form patty shapes, and pat into additional bread crumbs to coat. You can bake these on a non-stick cookie sheet or a piece of parchment paper laid on a cookie sheet for about 35 minutes at 375°. Turn once to brown both sides.

## LENTIL PATTIES
*Makes 4 to 6 patties.*

1 tbs. olive oil
1/2C chopped onion
1 clove of garlic, minced
1/2C grated carrots
1/2C grated mushrooms
1 tbs. tamari
1 tbs. thyme
1/4C mashed tofu
1 1/2C cooked lentils
1/2C bread crumbs or matzo meal

Heat oil in a skillet, and sauté onions and garlic for 6 minutes. Add carrots and mushrooms. Continue cooking for 3 more minutes and then add tamari and thyme. Stir well. Transfer ingredients to a bowl, and add the remaining ingredients. If the batter is too wet to form a "patty" shape, then add a bit more bread crumbs. Form patties, and lay them out on a parchment-lined cookie sheet. Bake for 25 minutes and then flip over. Bake for another 15 minutes.

Tastes great in a bun with slices of onion and tomato or with mushroom gravy. I sometimes make these for dinner and serve them with a big salad!

# SPREADS & DIPS

## PAPAYA CHUTNEY

2C chopped papaya
1/2C chopped sweet red pepper
1 1/2 tbsp. honey
1 1/2 tbsp. vinegar
3 tbsp. chopped fresh cilantro
1 tsp soy sauce
dash of cayenne
1/4 tsp cardamon
1C water

Combine all ingredients in a saucepan and simmer for 5 minutes. Serve hot or cold with braised vegetables or Indian pancakes.

# TOMATO RELISH

1/4 chopped green pepper

2 tomatoes fully finely chopped

1 small onion, minced

1/4 c finely chopped cilantro

1 garlic clove, minced

2 tbsp. vinegar

1/2 tsp. dry red pepper flakes

1 tsp. soy sauce

Combine all ingredients and allow to marinate for 4 hours before serving.

## TOFU SPREAD

*Makes 2 cups.*

Use a food processor for this spread. We like it smooth, but chunky also tastes great!

1C hard tofu
3 green onions chopped, (about 2/3C)
2 tbs. chopped green pepper
1 tsp. chopped fresh garlic
1/2 tsp. dry mustard
1/2 tsp. turmeric
1/2 tsp. soy sauce
1 tbs. miso paste
1 tsp. lemon juice

Blend all ingredients, and taste for seasonings. If you like a spicy dip, add more mustard and garlic. This spread makes a great start for a sandwich instead of mayonnaise. For instance: Spread tofu spread on one slice of bread and then add lettuce and tomato slices and/or soy cheese and soy bologna.

## RED PEPPER

Cut an opening in the base of 3 red peppers and discard the seeds. Roast over a flame until the skins are black. Put the peppers in a bowl to remove all of the charred skins. Chop the roasted peppers.

half pound tofu
2 cloves of roasted garlic
dash of cayenne or Tabasco® sauce
2 tbs. lemon juice
1 tsp. soy sauce
1 tbs. honey

Put all ingredients including the roasted peppers in a food processor, and purée until smooth. Wonderful in sandwiches with lettuce and sprouts. This is also great as a dip with celery and broccoli.

# MUSHROOM AND SUN DRIED TOMATO

Sauté in 1 tbs. olive oil for 5 minutes:

3 cloves of garlic, chopped
2C chopped mushrooms

Transfer to the bowl of the food processor, and add:

1/2 pound of tofu
1/2C sun dried tomatoes chopped
2 tbs. lemon juice
1/4C tomato puree
1 tbs. each: basil, oregano, and parsley

Purée until smooth. If this is too thick, add a little water or more tomato puree.

Delicious on sandwiches.

## CARROT TOFU SESAME

1 tbs. olive oil
1C chopped onions
2 cloves of garlic, minced
1/4C sesame seeds
2C cooked carrots (steamed)
half pound tofu
1/4C orange juice or lemon juice
1 tbs. soy sauce
1 1/2 tbs. honey

Sauté the first three ingredients until the onions are translucent. Add the sesame seeds, and sauté for 3 more minutes. Transfer to the bowl of a food processor, and add the remaining ingredients. Purée until smooth. To thin the spread, use a little liquid from the steamed carrots. Tasty sandwich spread.

## SKORDALIA

This is a Greek spread. It works well in sandwiches with lettuce and tomato. It can also be used as a dip for fresh vegetables. Skordalia makes a tasty sauce for rice too!

2C cubed boiled potatoes
1 1/2C cooked white beans (see Cooking Beans Chart)
1/4C lemon juice
liquid from beans or potatoes
1/4C chopped fresh parsley
2 cloves roasted garlic, minced
1 tbs. soy sauce
1/3C chopped walnuts or almonds

Purée the first three ingredients in a food processor. If it is too thick, add some liquid from the cooked beans or cooked potatoes.

In the food processor, add all the remaining ingredients. Purée until smooth. Add more liquid slowly, if necessary.

Skordalia will keep for 3 - 4 days covered and refrigerated.

# GREEN TAHINI

Combine in a blender:

1/2C tahini
1 tbs. lemon juice
1 tsp. tamari
pinch of cayenne pepper
1/4 - 1/2C water

When the tahini spread is smooth, add in the blender:

1/4C chopped arugola leaves
1/4C chopped parsley
1/2C chopped spinach

Blend together. This is a tasty sandwich spread that can be used with lettuce, tomato, cucumber, and sprouts.

# STOCKS, SOUPS, GRAVIES & SAUCES

## STOCKS AND SOUPS:
## SOME SUGGESTIONS

When making stock or soups, always make a large amount and freeze some in small containers for future use. Some soups, when puréed, make good sauces for pastas and rice dishes. And stocks are interchangeable most of the time. For instance, a lentil soup with mushroom stock will become a different soup with a vegetable stock or with soy milk added. Don't be afraid to experiment or try new combinations. All families are different, and tastes change. So try a variety until you hit on what seems to please your family the most.

# VEGETABLE STOCK

2C chopped onions
3 carrots cut into 2" pieces
2C chopped celery
4 cloves of garlic, scored*
1 parsnip
1/2C chopped green pepper
1/2C sherry
1 - 2 tbs. soy sauce
1 bay leaf
1/2C parsley sprigs
4 long fresh dill sprigs

In a large stock pot, combine the first eight ingredients. Cover generously with water. In a piece of cheese cloth, wrap the herbs and secure with a cotton thread. Place the herbs in the stock pot. Bring to a boil. Turn down the heat, and simmer for 1 1/2 hours, partially covered.

Cool slightly. Remove all vegetables and the cheese cloth by straining the liquid through a sieve into a bowl or pot. Divide the stock amongst 1 pint containers and freeze. This stock will last a month in the freezer. Don't forget to label and date the containers!

* To score garlic, make marks on the cloves with a knife. This helps the juice come out.

## MUSHROOM STOCK

Wash mushrooms first. Fill a large pot 3/4 of the way with button mushrooms. Pour purified water over the mushrooms, and fill the pot with the water. Bring to a boil.

Turn down the flame, and simmer for 1 1/2 hours uncovered. Let it cool and then strain the mushrooms reserving the liquid. This is mushroom stock. You can freeze it in small containers or keep the stock in the refrigerator for 3 - 4 days before using.

# BROWN STOCK

2 large baking potatoes, unpeeled and cut into pieces
2 large onions, peeled and cut into pieces
2 leeks or green onions, washed and cut into pieces
3 cloves of garlic, scored
2C whole button mushrooms
1 parsnip
1 1/2 tbs. soy sauce or tamari
10 peppercorns
1 bay leaf

Put all ingredients in a stock pot, cover with purified water, and bring to a boil. Lower heat, and simmer for 1 1/2 hours. Strain out vegetables and reserve them. The liquid is your stock. If you wish to thicken it, put some of the cooked potatoes and onion in the blender with a little stock and purée.

Add this mixture to the rest of the stock. Divide the stock into pint containers and freeze. I do this once a month and then have ready-to-use home-made stock on hand!

NOTE: The potatoes can also be served as a side dish. Sometimes I purée them with a little unflavored soy milk for a smooth mashed potato.

# MISO STOCK

*Serves 2 to 4.*

Miso is fermented soy bean paste. It comes either as rice miso, barley miso, or soy miso. Soy miso has the darkest color. Miso has a salty taste. It can be found in health food stores and some supermarkets in the oriental food department. It stays fresh in the refrigerator for a long time. I use it to flavor soups. Boiling miso destroys certain enzymes that aid in digestion, so only simmer this stock or add the miso after the stock is rich and cooked.

For a quick "stock -soup," combine in a medium size pot:

2 small carrots cut into 1/4" cubes
2 stalks of celery, chopped
2 green onions chopped (include the green part too!)
1 clove of garlic, minced
a dash of pepper
1/4C cubed tofu cut into 1/2" cubes (for soup only)

Simmer for 15 - 20 minutes. Add 1 - 2 tablespoons of miso and 1 teaspoon of soy sauce. For soup, just serve warm. For stock, quadruple the recipe. You can freeze this, but it takes so little time to prepare, that I just make it when I need it. My daughter loves it as a freshly-made soup.

NOTE: Add cooked pearl barley, short grain rice, or pasta for a fast soup and a hearty meal.

# SOY WHITE SAUCE

1C lite soy milk (unflavored)
1/4 - 1/3C whole wheat flour
1/2 tsp. soy sauce

Slowly heat soy milk and add whole wheat
flour while stirring constantly. Add soy sauce, and
stir until thick. Turn off heat so as not to burn sauce.
This is a basic sauce to which you can add wine,
vegetables, nuts, seeds, beans, potatoes or stock.

# MUSHROOM GRAVY

1 1/2C soy milk (unflavored)
3 tbs. unbleached or whole wheat flour
1/2 tsp. soy sauce
2 tbs. white wine
2C sliced mushrooms
1 tbs. olive oil
dash of white ground pepper
1 C vegetable stock

In a saucepan bring the soy milk to a boil. Add the flour and whisk until thick. Add the soy sauce. Slowly add the white wine while whisking. Keep whisking until thick, then set aside. In a skillet, sauté the mushrooms in the olive oil for 4 minutes. Add the stock, and sprinkle a little pepper into the sauce.

# MEXICAN SAUCE

In a sauce pan add:

2C tomato sauce (see page 203)
1/4C cilantro leaves
1/2C chopped green onions
2 cloves of garlic, chopped
dash of Tabasco® sauce
1 tsp. soy sauce

Cook on low heat for 1/2 hour. Serve hot over Mexican Crepes. (See Mexican Crepe recipe in Entrée This sauce will keep for 5 days in the refrigerator or will freeze well for 2 months.

## Blender Friendly Sauces

## WHITE SAUCE WITH BEANS
(Terrific on rice, vegetables or pastas)

1C soy milk
1C white beans cooked
1 - 2 garlic cloves, minced
1 tsp. dried dill weed
1 tsp. soy sauce
1/2C vegetable stock
1/4C sherry (after the alcohol is cooked out)
dash of white pepper
dash of nutmeg

Heat slowly in a saucepan until thick. Purée in blender for a smooth sauce.

## BROCCOLI PEANUT SAUCE
(great on bread or Soba noodles)

Steam enough broccoli to yield 2C when cooked and chopped.

Purée in blender:

2C cooked broccoli
2 tsp. peanut butter
1/2C soy milk

# TAHINI AND LENTIL SAUCE

Purée until finely chopped:

1/2C toasted almonds
1/2C sunflower seeds
1/4C pine nuts
1 1/2 - 2C cooked lentils
1 tbs. soy sauce

Then add slowly:

1/4C tahini
1/2 - 1C soy milk
1/4 tsp. nutmeg

If you want to use this as a sauce, add more liquid. If you want it as a spread, cut down on the amount of soy milk. As a sauce, a dash of sherry with the alcohol cooked out is a nice addition.

# SWEET AND SOUR SAUCE

Stir in a saucepan and simmer for 10 minutes:

12 oz. can of crushed pineapple with juice or
2C chopped fresh pineapple with juice
1 tbs. soy sauce or tamari
1/2C white wine vinegar
1" piece of ginger root, sliced into thirds
1 tbs. honey

Meanwhile, dissolve by stirring with a fork:

2 tbs. arrowroot flour
1/2C cold water

Slowly pour the arrowroot mixture into the cooking sauce while stirring. When this thickens, turn off the heat. If the sauce becomes too thick, you can thin it with orange juice.

## SOY NUT SAUCE

1/3C  sesame seeds
1/3C sunflower seeds
2C soy milk
3 - 4 tbs. unbleached flour
1 tsp. tamari
1/2 tsp. granulated garlic

Toast seeds in the oven until brown. Cool
seeds and then blend them into a coarse pulp. Set
aside. Bring soy milk to boil, and add flour, whisking
until thick. Turn down heat to simmer, and add
tamari, garlic, and seeds. Cook for another minute or
two and then remove from heat. This sauce is
wonderful on rice with pine nuts.

# RAISIN WINE SAUCE

1/2C orange juice
1/2C dry red wine
1/2C water
1/4C seedless raisins
1/4C honey
3 tbs. cornstarch
3 tbs. water
1 tbs. dry mustard

Combine the first five ingredients in a saucepan and simmer. Meanwhile, mix corn starch and water until dissolved, and then add dry mustard. Slowly add to the wine sauce. Stir until thickened.

## SPICY RED CHILI SAUCE

3C chopped, tomatoes
4 garlic cloves
1 jalapeno pepper, seeded (if you really like
   spicy, hot foods, include the seeds)
2 medium size onions, chopped
1/4C tomato paste or purée
1 tbs. cumin
1 tbs. coriander
1 tbs. tamari
2 tbs. chopped cilantro

In a food processor or blender, purée all the
ingredients until smooth. This spicy sauce mixed
with flat noodles is a nice addition to a meal of
vegetable patties and salad.

# BARBECUE SAUCE

16 oz. can of crushed tomatoes
2 tbs. molasses
1/4C cider vinegar
1/4C honey
1 tbs. soy sauce
1 tbs. prepared mustard
2 -3 drops of Tabasco® sauce
1/4 tsp. granulated garlic

Heat all of the ingredients in a saucepan, and simmer until they are combined. This will keep for keep for 5 days covered in the refrigerator.

## MISO SOUP

*Serves 4.*

1C chopped onions
2C raw chopped cabbage
1/2C chopped carrots
1/2C chopped celery
1/4C minced green onions
1 clove of garlic, minced
1 1/2C purified water

5C purified water
1/4C (4 tbs.) miso paste
1 tbs. soy sauce

Combine the first seven ingredients in a soup pot, and cover. Steam for 15 minutes. Uncover, and add the remaining ingredients. Do not boil. Simmer for 15 - 20 minutes more. Serve hot, and garnish with chopped parsley.

# CLEAR SOUP WITH MUSHROOMS
### *Serves 4 - 6.*

Wash and cut stems off of 2 ounces of Chinese dried black mushrooms.  Pour 2 c boiling water over them, and let them sit for 1/2 hour.  Drain and reserve liquid.  Cut the mushrooms into slices. Set aside.

Meanwhile, in a large pot, combine:

2 onions, cut in quarters
3 scallions, whole
1 to 2 inch piece of ginger, cut in half lengthwise
2 carrots, washed & whole
4 stalks of celery, whole
4 sprigs of parsley
1 sprig of fresh dill
2 garlic cloves, cut in half
3 c whole button mushrooms

Add enough water to cover, plus 3 c more. Bring to a boil. Turn down heat and simmer, partially covered,for 2 hours. Then remove the lid, and carefully strain the liquid into another pot. To the clear liquid, add the black mushrooms with:

*Continues...*

1 tbsp soy sauce
1/2 tsp white ground pepper
1/2 c chopped scallions
1/4 c dry sherry
1/2 tsp sesame oil (optional)

Simmer for 30 minutes longer, and serve with brown rice or  noodles.

## VEGETABLE SOUP

*Makes 1 gallon.*

Everyone has favorite vegetables, and vegetable soup has many variations. It's a good idea to start with onions, garlic, carrots, celery, and a parsnip, and then to add in your favorite seasonal vegetables. Here is a sample of a basic soup. Add your choices, always remembering to pour in more liquid (water or stock) and to adjust the seasonings.

> 2 large onions, chopped
> 4 carrots, chopped
> 6 celery stalks or one small bunch, chopped
> 1 parsnip whole (discard this when the soup is finished)
> 4 tomatoes, chopped
> 1/2C green pepper, chopped
> 6 cloves of garlic, chopped
> 2 tbs. soy sauce
> 1 bay leaf
> 1/4 tsp. group white pepper
> 1 tsp. dried basil
> 1C chopped zucchini
> 1C chopped sweet potato
> 1C chopped russet or Idaho potato

*Continues...*

In a 6 quart pot, add all of the ingredients. Add
water, filling the pot to at least 2 inches above the top
of the vegetables.

Bring to a boil, then turn flame down to
simmer. Cook for 1 1/2 hours until all vegetables are
tender. Remove parsnip. Taste, and adjust seasoning.

If you desire a thick soup, purée some vegetables in the blender and pour it back into the pot. This
thick soup also makes a great sauce for Vegetable
Risotto (see recipe in Entrée Section).

## TOMATO SOUP

6C fresh chopped tomatoes
1 tbs. granulated garlic
2C vegetable stock
1 tsp. miso paste
1/2 tsp. dried dill
1/2 tsp. dried basil leaves
1 bay leaf

Bring all ingredients to a boil in a soup pot.

Turn down heat and simmer for 45 minutes uncovered. Purée in a blender or food processor.

Add a little soy milk to several batches if you wish to make "cream of tomato" soup. Garnishing can be imaginative too. For example, try large croutons or an herb mix of parsley, chopped spinach, and scallions for example.

# TOMATO BARLEY SOUP

*Serves 4.*

1C cooked barley
3C chopped tomatoes
(Italian plum are the best when available)
1 small can tomato paste
1 tbs. basil
1 basil leaf
1 tsp. granulated garlic
1C mushroom stock

Prepare barley (see Cooking Grains chart on page 15) Combine all of the ingredients except the barley in a soup pot, and bring to a boil. Turn down heat, and simmer for 1hour. If the soup seems too thick, add a little more stock or purified water. Add the cooked barley just before serving.

This makes a hearty meal when served with black bread.

# WATERCRESS SOUP

*Serves 4.*

1 onion, chopped
1C celery leaves
2C watercress leaves
2 cloves garlic, minced
1 whole carrot
1 tbs. soy sauce
1/4C sherry
1/2 tsp. dill weed
dash of white pepper
6C vegetable stock
soy milk, unflavored

Simmer all ingredients (except soy milk) in vegetable stock for 1/2 hour. Remove carrot, and reserve. Purée the soup in a blender, adding in 1 - 2 tablespoon soy milk with each batch. You'll have about 3 - 4 batches in all. Return puréed soup to another soup pot until all is thickened. Cut carrot into small pieces, and add to thick soup. Heat gently, and serve hot.

# BORSCHT

*Serves 4 - 6.*

6C grated or chopped beets
6C water
1C vegetable stock
1C chopped carrots
1C chopped onions
1 tbs. soy sauce

Combine all ingredients in a soup pot, and bring to a boil. Turn down heat, and simmer for 1 hour. Add more liquid if necessary. When you turn off the heat add:

2 baked potatoes, cut into large pieces and cooled
1 tbs. vinegar
1 tbs. honey

Stir well, and serve hot.

For cold borscht, strain out all the vegetables and then add the vinegar and honey. Do not add the potatoes.

For a "cream" soup, add the cold borscht to the blender (small amounts at one time) with 1/4 to 1/3 cup of soy milk or non-fat yogurt and purée.

On a hot summer day, it's a wonderful chilled drink with lunch.

# CABBAGE SOUP

1 tbs. canola oil
3 large onions, chopped
3 garlic cloves, minced
2C chopped celery
1C yellow pepper chopped
2 1/2C white cabbage, chopped
1 small bok choy (Chinese cabbage), chopped
3C sliced mushrooms
3 tbs. rice vinegar
3 tbs. sherry
2 tbs. honey
6C vegetable stock
2C mushroom stock
1 tbs. tamari (Japanese soy sauce)
1 tbs. dried dill weed

In a soup pot, combine the first four ingredients and sauté for 8 minutes. Add the next four ingredients, and stir well. Cook for 8 more minutes, and add all the remaining items. Taste seasoning and adjust. Adding short grain brown rice to this soup makes for a really hearty meal. Simmer covered for 30 minutes. Serve hot.

# HEARTY BEAN SOUP

*Serves 6 to 8.*

The night before, soak 2 c white beans in a large saucepan in a cool place. The next morning, drain the water and fill the pot with fresh water. Cook for 1 1/2hours until beans are tender. Save the liquid.

2 onions, chopped
3 carrots, chopped
2 c chopped celery
3 cloves of garlic, chopped
1 large ripe tomato, chopped
1 parsnip, washed and whole
2 potatoes, chopped with the skins on
3 c vegetable stock
1 c bean broth
1/4 c parsley, chopped
1 tbsp chervil
Soy sauce to taste
1/2 tsp. black pepper
1 bay leaf

Combine all ingredients and cover w/water. Cook for 1 hour. Remove the parsnip, add the cooked beans, and continue cooking for another hour. If you need more liquid, add some bean broth or boiling water. Serve hot with warm bread. This is a hearty soup and can be considered the main dish of your meal!

## PEA SOUP

2C split green peas
1 carrot, cut into pieces
2 stalks of celery, whole
1 parsnip, washed and whole
1 large onion, cut in half
2 cloves of garlic, minced
6C purified water
1 tbs. soy sauce

Combine all of the ingredients in a soup pot. Cover and bring to a boil. Uncover and simmer for about 40 minutes more. Before serving, remove celery, parsnip, and onion if desired.

# SWEET LENTIL SOUP

*Serve 3 - 4.*

1 sweet potato, chopped
2 onions, chopped
1 clove of garlic, minced
1 cup  sliced mushrooms
1 cup chopped zucchini or yellow squash
1 cup tomato purée or 1 1/2 cup diced tomatoes
1/2 tsp. dried basil
1 tbs. parsley
1 tsp. soy sauce
dash of cayenne
dash of crushed red pepper
1 1/2C dried lentils

Combine all the ingredients in a stock pot, and cover with water.  Bring to a boil and then turn down heat to simmer.  Cook for about 45 minutes, stirring occasionally.

Don't let the liquid boil out.  Vegetable stock or more water can always be added.  Serve hot.

## WHITE BEAN OR NAVY BEAN SOUP

2C cooked white beans or navy beans
1 1/2 quart vegetable soup (see page 80)

Add beans to vegetable soup. Simmer for 1/2 hour. Add 2 tbs. of fresh parsley.

## KIDNEY BEAN SOUP

2C cooked kidney beans
1 1/2 quart vegetable soup (see page 80)

Add kidney beans to vegetable soup.

While simmering add:

2 cups chopped  tomato
1/4C chopped cilantro
1 tsp. jalapeno pepper chopped, finely (optional)

Cook for 35- 45 minutes.  Garnish with a dollop of non-fat yogurt.

## SWEET POTATO OR YAM SOUP

2 chopped, onions
6 yams or sweet potatoes, washed well with skins on
    and diced.
1 small apple, skinned, cored, and chopped
2C clear vegetable stock
6 - 8C water
1 tbs. soy sauce
dash of nutmeg
1 tsp coriander

Combine all the ingredients in a stock pot, and simmer uncovered for 40 minutes. Cool for 1/2 hour.

Purée in batches in the blender or food processor until all the soup is smooth.

Serve with thin crisp crackers with soy cheese melted on top. Tastes great together!

# POTATO AND CARROT SOUP

*Serves 4.*

1 tbs. canola oil
1C chopped leeks (washed well)
2 cloves garlic, minced
1 medium size onion, chopped
1/4C celery leaves, chopped
6C purified water
2C cubed potatoes, unpeeled
1C chopped carrots
1/2 tsp. dried dill weed
1/2C dry sherry
1 tbs. soy sauce or tamari

    Sauté in the oil the next four ingredients. When the onions are translucent, add all of the remaining ingredients. Bring to a boil. Turn down heat, and simmer for 1 1/2 hours covered. Allow to cool slightly and then purée 1 cupful at a time with 1/4C soy milk to thicken.
    When all the soup is puréed, heat slowly.
    Serve hot garnished with grated carrots and chopped parsley.

## CURRIED CARROTS AND POTATOES WITH QUINOA SOUP

1 tbs. safflower oil
1 clove garlic, minced
1/2C green onions, chopped
1 tsp. mustard seeds
1 tsp. tumeric
1/2 - 1 tsp. curry paste
   (found in health food stores)
dash of mace* or nutmeg
1C diced carrots
1/2C chopped onions
1C chopped potatoes (1/4" cubes)
1/2C corn kernels
4C vegetable stock
1 tsp. soy sauce

   Combine the first four ingredients in a soup pot. Heat and stir until the seeds begin to pop. Add the tumeric and curry paste. Stir well and then add all of the remaining ingredients. Make sure the liquid covers the vegetables. Purified water or more stock can always be added. Simmer for 1 hour. Allow to cool slightly and then puree in batches in the blender. Serve with cooked quinoa (see chart page 15).

   * Mace adds an interesting flavor to the soup. It comes from the skin of nutmeg.

## PISTOU SOUP

1/2 lg. onion coarsely chopped
2 carrots, cut into 1/2" chunks
2 leeks, washed well, with some greens, cut
   into 1/2" pieces
2 celery stalks with leaves, cut into 1/2" pieces
3 saffron threads
4-1/2C water or vegetable bouillon
1 lb chopped tomatoes
2 med size zucchini, chopped
2C cooked kidney beans
3C vegetable broth
1 tbsp soy sauce
1C cooked brown rice

In a large pot, bring the first six ingredients to a boil. Turn down heat and simmer for just 15 minutes. Add the tomatoes and zucchini and continue cooking for 15 minutes. Add the beans, remaining stock and soy sauce. Simmer for 20 more minutes and then add the cooked rice.

*Continues...*

Prepare pistou in a small bowl by pressing with a fork:

1 1/2 tsp chopped garlic
dash of salt
2 tsp chopped basil
1/2 tsp olive oil
1/4 c tomato paste

Add the pistou slowly to the soup, stirring until all is combined.

Serve hot.  (This soup does not freeze well.)

# BUTTERNUT SQUASH SOUP

1 10" long butternut squash

Peel the butternut squash. Cut and remove seeds and "threads". Cube and then boil for 10 - 12 minutes. Drain water, and set aside.

In a medium soup pot add:

4C vegetable stock
1C cubed carrots
1/2C chopped apple
1C chopped onion

Bring to a boil, turn down the heat, and simmer for 15 minutes. Add cooked squash and:

a dash of cinnamon
pinch of nutmeg
1 tsp. tamari

Cook for 10 more minutes and then let cool for 10 minutes.

Blend in batches. If you wish a creamier consistency, add 2 - 3 tbs. unflavored soy milk with each batch. Garnish with a dash of cinnamon.

# SALADS

# GREEN SALAD WITH SPROUTS

Salads are a special part of any meal, and you can vary them endlessly. There are a number of new lettuces, cabbages, and wild greens available in the market. For example, you can find dandelion and wild mustard greens, lambs lettuce, bib, red romaine and green romaine, red leaf and green leaf, red butter lettuce, arugala (which is high in calcium), raddichio, and green and red cabbages.

Experiment with interesting vinegars like balsamic, blueberry, raspberry, wine, tarragon, cider, and rice vinegar.

You only need to use a hint of oil. Learn to eat greens for their own taste, and use less dressing.

Garnish with sprouts! There are many kinds of sprouts, and they are easy to grow. Here's how: use a jar with a wide neck, put 1/2 c lentils (or mung beans, alfalfa seeds, or sunflower seeds) in the jar, and cover with purified water. Cut a piece of cheese cloth to fit generously over the jar's neck, and secure it with a rubber band. Let the beans or seeds soak for 1hour, then pour out the water through the cheese cloth.

*Continues...*

Shake the jar gently to distribute the seeds as evenly as possible, and let the jar sit on its side in a shady place.

We like to keep them out on the kitchen counter, near the sink – but out of the direct sun. Wet the seeds, and pour out the water 3 or 4 times a day. You don't have to soak them again. Some beans sprout in 48 hours; some take a few more days.

When the sprouts have little green tips, eat them! Put them in a container in the refrigerator. They will last 5 days.

# CAESAR SALAD WITH CROTOUNS

Chop and then chill romaine lettuce. Toast whole wheat bread, and let it stand for 10 minutes.

Cut toast into cubes.

DRESSING

In a jar, mix and shake well:

2 tsp. olive oil
2 cloves garlic, crushed
1/4 c lemon juice
1 tbsp soy sauce
2 tbsp soy milk

Toss dressing with lettuce, and add croutons and a small amount of grated soy cheese.

## TOSSED SPINACH SALAD

*Serves 4.*

1 bunch of spinach leaves
   (washed until all dirt and sand are gone)
1 small head of butter lettuce leaves, rinsed
1 C of chopped celery
1/4 C chopped yellow pepper
3/4 C sliced mushrooms
1/2 C alfalfa sprouts

   Combine the first five ingredients, and toss with Mustard Vinaigrette (See page 133) or Lemon Dill dressing (See page 132). Top with alfalfa sprouts.

# PURPLE CABBAGE SALAD

*Serves 4 - 6.*

In a bowl combine:

2C shredded purple cabbage
1C shredded Chinese cabbage
1/4C sliced thin radishes
1/4 C chopped green onions
2C romaine lettuce, shredded
1C shredded carrots
1/2C corn kernels

Combine in a salad bowl, and toss with Spicy Vinegar Dressing (See page 129).

# CABBAGE SALAD

*Serves 4 - 6.*

2C red cabbage, shredded
3C green cabbage, shredded
1C grated carrots
1C chopped celery
1/4C chopped green onions
1 1/2C mung bean sprouts

Combine all the vegetables, and toss gently. In a separate bowl, whisk together the dressing.

1/4 C water
1/2 C red wine vinegar
1/4 C dry sherry
2 tbsp honey
2 cloves garlic, minced
1/2 tsp soy sauce
1 tsp dried dill weed

Pour the dressing over the vegetables, and serve chilled on a bed of romaine lettuce or a large fresh cabbage leaf.

Note: This salad is wonderful as filling for a sandwich in a "hero roll" with grated soy cheese and soy bologna.

# SPROUT AND CABBAGE SALAD

1 tbs. honey
2 tbs. fresh lime juice
2 tbs. almond nut butter
1/4C water
1/4C unflavored soy milk


1C mung bean sprouts
1C sunflower seed sprouts
1 head bok choy, shredded in thick pieces
1 head Napa cabbage, shredded in thin pieces

Prepare dressing first by combining the first five ingredients until the nut butter is dissolved. Use a blender or whisk. Set aside.

In a bowl, combine the sprouts. In a steamer basket, place both cabbages and steam for just 3 minutes. You don't want them to wilt. Remove from heat, and run under cold water. Toss the sprouts and cabbages together and then toss with the dressing.

## CUT VEGETABLE SALAD WITH WARM TORTILLAS

3 carrots, chopped
1 bunch of celery, chopped
1/4 head purple cabbage, chopped
1 yellow squash, coarsely grated
6 medium mushrooms, sliced
2 medium tomatoes, seeded* and chopped
1c broccoli flowerets with some stem, chopped
3 scallions, chopped (also called green onions)

Combine all of the above ingredients in a salad bowl.

1/3 c balsamic vinegar
1 tsp. granulated garlic or two cloves of mincedfresh garlic
1 tsp. dried dillweed
a dash of ground pepper
1/4 c chopped parsley
1/4 c water

*Continues...*

Mix the second group of ingredients together in a bowl with a whisk or shake well in a jar. Pour the dressing over the vegetables, and then toss the salad. Serve with warmed tortillas which can be eaten separately or wrapped around portions of the salad.

*To seed the tomatoes: cut them in half and scoop out all of the seeds, leaving as much of the tomato intact as possible.

# ORIENTAL TOFU SALAD

*Serves 4.*

1 lb. block of tofu, cubed into 1/4" pieces

Toss with:

1/2C chopped green pepper
1/2C chopped green onions
1 1/2C mung bean sprouts
1 1/2C shredded Chinese cabbage
1C shredded romaine lettuce
1C shredded carrots

Combine all the vegetables and tofu, and then prepare dressing by mixing in a jar:

1 tbs. canola oil
1 tbs. sesame oil
6 - 8 tbs. rice vinegar
1 tbs. soy sauce
dash of cayenne
1 crushed garlic clove
1" slice of ginger (to be removed after dressing is made)
1 tsp. miso paste

Shake well. Pour over salad, and toss gently. Top with toasted sesame seeds, and serve chilled.

# AVOCADO AND TOFU SALAD

*Serves 4.*

1C grated carrots
1C tofu, cubed into 1/4" pieces
1C chopped celery
1/4C green onion
1/4C chopped red pepper

In a bowl, combine all of the ingredients. Arrange spinach or lettuce leaves to form a nest, and put carrot mix in center.

Slice:
1/2 avocado

Arrange avocado around the center. Make dressing in a jar and shake well:

1 tbs. olive oil
3 tbs. balsamic vinegar
1 tsp. dry dill weed
1 tsp. granulated garlic or minced fresh garlic
dash of pepper

Pour dressing over salad, and top with:

1/4C sunflower seeds
2 tbs. golden raisins

## SOUTH OF THE BORDER TOFU SALAD

3 tomatoes, chopped
1 lb. cake of tofu, cubed into 1/4" pieces
2 green onions (white and green parts), chopped
1 peeled cucumber, diced
1 yellow pepper, chopped

Combine all of the ingredients in a mixing bowl. Prepare dressing by whisking together:

1 tbs. olive oil
3 tbs. red wine vinegar
2 tbs. chopped cilantro
1 clove of garlic, crushed
dash of freshly ground black pepper
1/2 tsp crushed chili peppers

Pour over vegetables, and top with your favorite sprouts.

## MARINATED BEAN SALAD

When I lived in New York I used to get a "Hero" sandwich with marinated vegetables, bean salad, and shredded lettuce. It was great!

Overnight, soak the following beans in enough water to cover them and then some.

1/2 C kidney beans
1/2 C chick peas
1/2 C navy beans
1/2 C pinto beans

The next day, drain the water. Add new water, and cook until soft – about 1 - 1 1/2 hours. Drain off liquid (it can be used in soup stock later, just freeze it!). Put cooked beans in a bowl to cool. Make a marinade in another large bowl, large enough to put ALL the beans.

1 C red wine vinegar
1/2 C apple cider vinegar
1 - 2 tsp. honey
1 tbs. tamari
1/3 C purified water
1 bay leaf                          *Continues...*

1 tsp. dill weed
1/4 tsp. white ground pepper
1 C chopped celery
1/2 C minced onion
1/8 C chopped garlic

Mix marinade well and then pour on beans. Toss gently and well. Wax beans or green beans are also a nice addition. Toss the beans in the marinade and then cover and refrigerate overnight. Mix the beans several times during the refrigeration to make sure they all get marinated.

*Ideas:*

1. *Marinated beans with a green salad are a nice touch.*

2. *Grated carrots and zucchini mixed with the beans are a refreshing salad.*

3. *Beans mashed onto a piece of toast add something different to a meal.*

# MARINATED SALAD

1 c grated carrots
1 c chopped celery
1 c cauliflower pieces
1/2 c chopped green onions
1 c sliced mushrooms
1 1/2 c chopped red cabbage
1/2 c chopped jicama or sliced water chestnuts

Prepare all the vegetables, and combine in a salad bowl. Set aside, and whisk together the dressing ingredients:

1/4 c balsamic vinegar
2 tsp minced garlic
1 tsp dried dill weed
2 tbsp water
2 tbsp chopped parsley

Pour the dressing over the salad, and gently toss. Garnish with tomato wedges and your favorite sprouts.

Sometimes I grate soy cheese and top the salad with it!

# CORN AND BEAN SALAD

1 c cooked black beans
1 c corn kernels
1/4 c chopped red pepper
1/4 c chopped green pepper
1/2 c grated carrot
1/2 c chopped celery
1/4 c chopped green onion
1/3 c balsamic vinegar
2 cloves garlic, chopped
1/4 c chopped parsley
1 tbsp dill weed
1/2 tsp. soy sauce

Prepare black beans as in bean chart. Drain off liquid. Combine first seven ingredients gently. In a bowl, whisk together the remaining ingredients, and then gently combine the dressing with the vegetables.

Clean romaine lettuce leaves, and arrange them on a plate to form a nest. Spoon out salad, and serve chilled.

# RICE AND BEAN SALAD

Overnight, soak covered in water:
1C kidney beans
1C black beans
1C soy beans

In the morning pour off the water. Add new water to cover and then cook until tender – about 1 1/2 hours.  Set aside.

1 1/2 C short grain brown rice
1/2 C wild rice

Cook all rice in 4C purified water until boiling. Cover and turn down heat to simmer for 35 - 45 minutes. Turn off heat: Do not uncover for at least 10 minutes.

1C chopped celery
1 small onion, chopped
1 C shredded carrots

Toss rice, beans, and vegetables together.

*Continues...*

Prepare dressing by combining in a jar:

1/2C red wine vinegar
2 tbs. lemon juice
1/2 tsp. granulated garlic
1 tsp. soy sauce
1 tsp. honey
1/2 tsp. dill weed
pepper to taste
1/4C water

Toss all ingredients with dressing, and serve on a large leaf of romaine lettuce. Garnish with mung bean (This will last 2 - 3 days in refrigerator, but because of lemon juice will not last much longer.)

This makes a tasty dish to pack for lunch along with some hearty bread.

# TOMATO AND BEAN SALAD

2 large tomatoes
1C. soy cheese
2C marinated beans
4 tbs. chopped parsley

On a cookie sheet lined with parchment paper, lay 8 slices of tomato 1/4" thick. Top each slice with grated soy cheese and broil for 6 - 8 minutes until cheese melts. Remove from broiler, and on 4 separate plates, place 2 tomato slices side by side. Top with marinated beans (see page 113) and chopped parsley.

## SPICY LENTIL SALAD

1 1/4C dried lentils

Wash the dried lentils. Cook in enough water to cover. Simmer until tender, not soft and mushy. Drain off all water, rinse in cold water, and set aside to cool.

In a small bowl, whisk together and set aside:

3 tbs. red wine vinegar
1 1/2 tbs. safflower oil
1/2 tsp. soy sauce
1/2 tsp. freshly ground black pepper
1/3C chopped shallots
1/4 C chooped cilantro

Wash and seed 2 hot chilies. Always remember when handling chilies to wear rubber gloves and not to touch your face. Wash chilies in cold water. Remove seeds and stems and any large seams inside the chili. Cut into long strips and then cut into 1 inch slices. Add the chilies to the marinade and stir.
Now add the chilled lentils and combine well. Allow the lentils to marinate for at least an hour.
Tastes wonderful served with black bread!

## ANTIPASTO SALAD

Everybody likes to pick and taste, so here's an opportunity to treat the family to a fun appetizer. It may seem like work at first, but after a while you can serve leftovers plus condiments.

For example, an antipasto might consist of:

carrot and celery sticks
artichoke hearts
 or quartered freshly cooked artichokes
marinated roasted peppers*
cherry tomatoes
avocado slices
cold, cooked asparagus spears
marinated mushrooms and eggplant cubes*
marinated broccoli and cauliflower*
soy cheese slices
soy bologna slices
bean dip

Arrange on a large platter, and garnish with parsley.  Serve with toasted sourdough bread.

* Recipes on next page

# *MARINATED ROASTED PEPPERS

Before marinating the peppers, core and seed them.

Then, roast the peppers on an open flame on the stove – or under the broiler – until charred. Let cool and then peel off all burnt skins which are great for compost. Slice the peppers in eighths, and marinate in balsamic vinegar for 1/2 hour.

Refrigerate covered. The peppers will keep for several days.

They're also great chopped up in salad.

# *MARINATED MUSHROOMS AND EGGPLANT CUBES

To make a warm marinade for the mushrooms and eggplant cubes (or broccoli and cauliflower), place the following ingredients in a frying pan:

1 c water
6 peppercorns
3 cloves of garlic, sliced
1/2 c dry sherry
1 tbsp soy sauce (optional)
1/4 c lemon juice
1 bay leaf
1/2 piece of fresh ginger (optional)

Bring to a boil, and then turn down the heat. Add the vegetables – a few at a time – and simmer for 6 to 10 minutes. Do not overcook. Remove the vegetables with a slotted spoon and refrigerate. (The vegetables are also a great snack with crackers.)

## TABOULIE

I know this appears in every cookbook, but it's such a good tasting refreshing salad that I decided to include it.

1C water
dash of salt
1C dry bulgar wheat

Boil the salted water. Add the bulgar wheat and cover the pot. Turn off the heat and let it stand <u>covered</u> for 15 - 20 minutes. Cool in the refrigerator.

In a separate bowl toss together:

1/2C chopped parsley
1/4C chopped mint
1C diced tomatoes
dash of salt and pepper
1/4C lemon juice

Toss in the bulgar wheat after it cools. You can add any number of favorite vegetables such as: grated carrots, diced broccoli, cucumbers, peppers, cauliflower, or celery. Be innovative and have fun!

# SALAD DRESSING

## VINAIGRETTE

1/4C orange juice
1 tsp. orange peel
3 tbs. brown rice vinegar
1 tbs. safflower oil
1 tsp. soy sauce
1/4 tsp. ginger juice or 3 very thin slices of fresh ginger
1 clove of garlic, minced

In a blender, combine all ingredients.

# SESAME VINAIGRETTE

1 tsp. sesame oil
1 tsp. soy oil
4 tbs. rice vinegar
1 tbs. honey
dash of cayenne
dash of soy sauce
1/4C water

In a blender, combine all ingredients.

## SPICY VINEGAR

1/2 C red wine vinegar
2 tbs. olive oil
1/8 tsp. cayenne pepper
1/8 tsp. basil leaves
1 clove of garlic, crushed
1/8 tsp. soy sauce

In a blender, combine all ingredients.

# CUCUMBER

3 cucumbers, peeled and diced

Marinate diced cucumbers overnight in:

1C red wine vinegar
1/4C purified water
2 tbs. honey
3 tbs. lemon juice
1/2 tsp. soy sauce
dash of powdered mustard
1/2 tsp. basil

The next day, in a blender add: the marinade, cucumbers and 2 tomatoes, seeded and chopped.

## SUMMER FRESH

1/2C orange juice
1/3C balsamic vinegar
1 1/2 tbs. olive oil
1/2 tsp. basil leaves, dried
1/2 tsp. soy sauce
dash of ground pepper

Mix all the ingredients in a jar, and shake well. Use this dressing within 2 days.

A butter lettuce and romaine salad with endive and walnuts tastes wonderful with this dressing.

## LEMON DILL

In a blender combine:

1/2 C lemon juice
2 tbs. olive oil
1 tbs. dried dill weed
1/8 tsp. soy sauce
1 tsp. granulated garlic or 1 clove minced
2 tbs. purified water

Blend for 30 seconds.
This dressing will keep in the refrigerator for 2 days.

# MUSTARD VINAIGRETTE

In a blender combine:

1/2C white wine vinegar
1 tbs. canola oil
1 tbs. olive oil
2 tbs. lemon juice
1 tbs. prepared mustard
1 tsp. dried dill weed
2 tbs. water
1 tbs. honey

Blend for 30 seconds.
This dressing will keep in the refrigerator for 2 days.

## TAHINI

In a blender combine:

1/2C tahini
2 tbs. lemon juice
1/2C water
1 tsp. soy sauce
1 tbs. dried dill weed
1 tsp. granulated garlic or 2 garlic cloves, minced
1 tbs. canola oil
2 tsp. cider vinegar

Blend on and off until all ingredients are combined.

## TOFU MAYONNAISE

This makes a wonderful base for creamy salad dressings.

1 lb. cubed tofu pieces
3 tbs. lemon juice
1/3C water
1 1/2 tbs. canola oil
1 1/2 tbs. miso
1 tsp. tamari

Blend all the ingredients until smooth. Add more water slowly if you want a thinner consistency.

For **1000 ISLAND DRESSING**: combine and blend well:

1/2C tofu mayonnaise
1/3C tomato sauce or ketchup

# FRENCH HERB DRESSING

Blend all ingredients until smooth.

1/2C tofu mayonnaise
1/4C lemon juice
1 tbs. dried dill weed
1 garlic clove, minced
2 tbs. dried parsley
1/2 tsp. thyme

## CREAMY HERB DRESSING

Blend the following until smooth.

1/2C tofu mayonnaise
1/4C red wine vinegar
1 tsp. dried dill weed
1 garlic clove, minced
1 tsp. prepared mustard
dash of black pepper

# DIJON MUSTARD

1/2C tofu mayonnaise
1/4C lemon juice
1/4C Dijon mustard
1 tsp. dried dill
juice from 2 cloves of garlic
dash of pepper
1 tbs. olive oil

Blend well until smooth.

## JAPANESE RADISH

1 medium size (8") Daikon (Japanese radish)
1 small onion, cut into pieces
2 tsp. soy sauce
2 tbs. rice vinegar
4 tbs. water
2 tbs. safflower oil

Blend until smooth, and serve over sprout salad.

# GREEN GODDESS

1/2 lb. tofu
1/2C chopped fresh spinach
1/4C chopped parsley
2 garlic cloves, minced
2 tbs. chopped green pepper
4 tbs. cider vinegar
1 tsp. chopped fresh basil
1/4C chopped arugola ( if available, if not substitute
green chard)
1/2C water
1 tbs. soy sauce
1/4 tsp. black pepper

Combine in a food processor until smooth.


This dressing will last about a week in the
refrigerator when covered tightly. It also makes a tasty
dip for vegetables in packed lunches and can be used as
a spread on sandwiches.

# ASIDES

## "ASIDES"

What is an "aside?" When you become a vegetarian you find it is not always necessary to build your
meal around a "main dish". In our home, we like to
eat salad and several aside dishes with a grain or beans.
Being able to buy such a variety of seasonal vegetables
as we can in California makes varying and combining
easy. If you live where summer vegetables are scarce in
winter, enjoy the roots and hearty vegetables that are
available. In the summer, can or freeze some summer
favorites and then enjoy them throughout the year. So
an 'aside' is a dish that you can introduce in a small
amount which can later become a main dish.

# ROASTED GARLIC

Roasted garlic can be eaten as is, used as a spread, or added as an ingredient in recipes. Once roasted, the garlic stays fresh in the refrigerator in a sealed container for about a week. Mine never last that long! Remove as much of the outer skin as possible without dividing up the whole head.

Brush just enough olive oil on the garlic, not a lot! Roast in the oven for 20 minutes at 375 ° Each clove can be individually opened and spread on a piece of bread.

## SALSA

3 ripe tomatoes, chopped coarsely
1/4 c chopped cilantro
2  green onions, chopped
1 clove of garlic, chopped
1 c tomato juice

Combine and toss. This can sit in the refrigerator for a few days, but it will get spicier as it sits.

# GUACAMOLE

2  avocados, seeded and peeled
1 tomato, sliced
1/4 C chopped onion
1 clove of garlic, chopped
dash of cayenne pepper
1 tbs. cilantro

Combine all the ingredients in a food processor. Turn food processor on and off until mixture is smooth. To keep fresh, put in an airtight container or press Saran Wrap® to the surface of the guacamole so no air touches it.

Guacamole does not last long, but it is quick to make.

*Variations:*
    *1. Add chopped green pepper.*
    *2. Chopped carrots and celery to make a chunky
        guacamole.*
    *3. Add hot sauce.*

# MUSHROOM CAVIAR

*Makes 2 1/2 Cups.*

2 tsp. olive oil
1/2C chopped onions
1/2C green onions, chopped
4 cloves of garlic, minced

3C grated mushrooms
1 tsp. dried thyme
1 - 2 tbs. soy sauce
1/4 tsp. white ground pepper

Sauté the first four ingredients for 8 minutes.

Add the mushrooms. Mix together well, and cook for 5 more minutes. Add the remaining ingredients, stir well, and cook in the juice for about 8 more minutes. With a slotted spoon, transfer the sauté to a food processor. Add just enough liquid from the pan so that it mixes easily.

Purée on and off a few times until the paté is like a coarse paste. The caviar will refrigerate well for up to 4 days. NOTE: This is a good addition to an antipasto.

Caviar also makes a good spread in a sandwich. As a paté, this goes well with toasted bread. For parties, mold on a plate and decorate with parsley and lemon twists.

147

# MARINATED MUSHROOMS

2 tbs. olive oil
1/2C water
juice of 2 lemons
2 cloves of garlic, chopped
1 tsp. peppercorns
1 bay leaf
1 tsp. soy sauce
2C button mushrooms

Combine all of the ingredients except mushrooms and simmer for 6 minutes. Add the mushrooms, and cook, stirring for 8 minutes.

Cool and strain off liquid. Chill in refrigerator.

These are great on an antipasto plate or as an addition to a salad.

# BEAN DIP

Cover 2 c dried pinto or black beans with purified water, and soak them overnight in a cool place. In the morning, drain the water. Cover the beans with fresh water, and cook for 1 1/2 hours until they are soft. Drain beans, and save liquid for use in soups. This stock can be frozen in easy-to-thaw-and-use portions.

2 tbsp. molasses
1/4 c honey
1/2 c tomato sauce
 cooked beans

In a saucepan, combine all the ingredients. Heat, stirring constantly. If the beans begin sticking to the pan,scrape the bottom with a wooden spoon.

(Metal utensils may scratch the bottom of a no-stick pan. Use wooden utensils for cooking whenever possible.) When the beans are soft and the liquid has turned "saucy" (in about 8 to 10 minutes), remove from heat.

Place refried beans in the blender with one chopped tomato and a dash of cayenne pepper. Blend until smooth.

Serve with no-oil chips or vegetable slices.

## LENTIL DIP

*Makes 2 1/2 cups.*

1 c green or red lentils
3 c purified water

Cook the ingredients in a saucepan for about 20 minutes until the lentils are soft. Drain off the excess water, and reserve it for use later in soups, etc.

1/2 tbsp canola oil
1/2 onion, chopped
2 cloves of garlic, minced
1 1/2C chopped tomato
1 tsp soy sauce or tamari
1 tsp thyme
dash of cayenne or Tabasco®

Heat oil. Add onions and garlic, and cook until onions are translucent. Add tomatoes, and sauté for 5 more minutes.

Add the rest of the ingredients, stir well, and turn off heat. Allow to cool slightly.

In a food processor, combine the lentils and the onion mix.

Purée until smooth. This recipe can be doubled and will keep well in the refrigerator for 4 to 5 days covered.

# TAHINI DIP

*Makes 2 1/2 cups.*

You can buy prepared tahini dip in health food stores, but here's a homemade variety made with garbanzos. ( much like humus.)

1 c cooked garbanzo beans
1/2 c garbanzo liquid (If you open a can, use the
    beans and liquid.  If you cook the beans, use
    the liquid in which the beans are cooked.)
1/2 c tahini (sesame paste)
1/2 tsp granulated garlic or 2 cloves pressed
    (use only juice from pressed garlic)
a dash of soy sauce
1/4 c toasted sesame seeds
1 tbsp lemon or lime juice

Blend all the ingredients in a food processor until smooth.  Serve the dip with cut-up vegetables such as carrots,celery, broccoli, and jicama.

## DAL

This Indian side dish tastes great with rice and Indian flat bread. It's easy to make and also spreads well on sandwiches.

3C cooked lentils in vegetable broth (see bean cooking chart, page 16)
5C vegetable broth
1 tbs. vegetable oil
1 tbs. mustard seeds
1-1/2 C chopped onions
2 cloves of garlic, minced
1 tsp. turmeric
1/2 of a chili pepper, seeded and chopped fine
1 tsp. ground cumin
1 tsp. tamari
1 1/2 C stewed chopped tomatoes
dash of coriander

Cook lentils in vegetable broth. Heat oil and sauté mustard seeds until they begin to pop. Add the onion and garlic and sauté for 5 minutes. Add all the remaining ingredients, including the cooked lentils. Simmer for 8 - 10 more minutes. Dal can be served either thick or thin. Adjust it to your liking.

# SOUTHERN BEANS

2 tbs. olive oil
1/2 onion, sliced
1 clove of garlic, minced

1C sliced mushrooms
2C collard greens (or spinach or chard)
1C cooked navy beans or pinto beans
  (see cooking chart on page 16)
1 tbs. tamari
dash of dill weed
dash of white pepper

    Sauté the first three ingredients until the onions are translucent. Add the mushroom and greens, and continue cooking for 3 more minutes. Add the cooked beans, and toss well to combine. Season with tamari, dill, and pepper, and serve hot.

# GREEN RICE

3C cooked brown rice
1 tbs. safflower oil
1 1/2C chopped onions
1/2C chopped green onions or leeks (washed well)
3 cloves of garlic, minced
1C chopped celery
1/2C chopped green pepper
1C shredded Swiss chard or spinach
1/4C minced fresh parsley
1/2 tsp. dill weed
1 tbs. soy sauce

Prepare brown rice.

In a wok, sauté the next four ingredients for 8 minutes. Then add the next five ingredients, and cook for 5 more minutes. Stir in the soy sauce. Add the brown rice, and toss well. Serve hot.

This dish is great with broccoli flowers also!

# SPANISH RICE

2 tbs. olive oil
1C chopped onions
1C chopped celery
1C grated carrots
1/2 jalapeno pepper, minced
3 cloves garlic, minced
1/2C chopped green pepper
1/2 tsp. red pepper flakes
1 tsp. paprika
1/2C minced cilantro leaves
1/4C minced parsley
1 tbs. wine vinegar
1 tsp. oregano
1 - 1 1/2 tbs. tamari
3C cooked brown rice
1 1/2 C chopped tomatoes
1/2C chopped green olives

In a skillet, sauté the first six ingredients until the onions are brown. Add the next five ingredients. Continue cooking for a few more minutes, and then add the vinegar, oregano, and tamari. Stir well, and add the cooked rice.

Now add the tomatoes and olives. Serve hot, garnished with chopped scallions and parsley.

## TANGY VEGETABLES

2C vegetable broth
2 medium onions, cut into chunks
3 carrots, cut into small round pieces
2 yellow squash, cut into 1/2" cubes
2C washed and chopped mustard greens or spinach
1 tbs. arrowroot
1/4C water
1 tsp. prepared mustard
1 tsp. tamari

Combine first four ingredients, and simmer for 10 minutes. Add the mustard greens or spinach, and continue cooking over a low heat. Stir together the arrowroot and water until dissolved and then add the prepared mustard and tamari. Add the arrowroot liquid to the hot vegetables, and stir until thickened.

Start this dish as a side dish with brown rice or basmati rice. It can eventually become a main course with a variety of different vegetables.

# VEGETABLE SQUASH PIE

5C steamed, cubed banana squash
1 tbs. canola oil
1 onion, diced
1/4C chopped green onion with tops
2 cloves of garlic, minced
1/2C diced zucchini
2 1/2C corn kernels (cooked)
1 tsp. soy sauce
1/2C corn meal

Purée all 5 cups of banana squash. Set aside.

Sauté onion and garlic in canola oil until the onions are translucent. Add the zucchini and corn, and continue cooking for 6 more minutes. Add the soy sauce. Combine well, and add the corn meal. Stir well, and turn off heat.

Pour in the puréed squash, and mix all ingredients well.

Pour into a Pyrex® baking dish, and bake at 350° for 30 minutes covered. Uncover and bake for 30 minutes more. Serve hot.

# EASTERN STYLE POTATOES

3C of sliced potatoes 1/4" cubes
1 tbs. safflower oil
1 tbs. mustard seeds
1 large onion, finely chopped
2 cloves of garlic, minced
medium size green pepper, chopped
1 tsp. turmeric
1/4 tsp. coriander
1/2 tsp. cumin
1 tbs. soy sauce
juice of 1 lemon
1/2C water or vegetable broth

Boil the potatoes for about 20 minutes until tender. Drain, and set aside. In a skillet, heat the oil and sauté the mustard seeds until they begin to pop. Add the onion and garlic, and continue stirring until the onion is translucent. Add the next five ingredients, and stir for 3 minutes. Add the potatoes, and toss well. Stir in the juice from one lemon and 1/2C water or vegetable broth. Cook for 10 minutes until all the flavors are combined. Serve hot.

# GREEK POTATOES

3 - 4 lbs. baking potatoes, cubed 1/2"
1 tsp. olive oil (preferably first press)
1C lemon juice
2 cloves garlic, minced
2 tsp. dried oregano
1/2C chopped green onion
1 tsp. soy sauce
dash of freshly ground black pepper

Boil potatoes for 20 minutes in enough water to cover them. Drain and set aside. In a wok, add all the other ingredients except the soy sauce and pepper. Add the potatoes and cook, stirring so the potatoes don't stick to the sides. Add soy sauce and pepper.
Serve hot garnished with chopped parsley.

# HASH BROWNS

2 lbs. cubed potatoes
2 tbs. canola oil
1 onion, chopped
2 cloves of garlic, minced
2 green onions, chopped
1 tbs. soy sauce
1 tbs. Tabasco®
1 tbs. paprika

Boil potatoes for 20 minutes until tender.
Drain and set aside. Sauté the next four ingredients until the onions are translucent and then add the cooked potatoes. Toss with soy sauce and Tabasco®, and cook for 10 minutes. Sprinkle with paprika before serving.

# POTATO SOUFFLÉ

*Serves 6 to 8.*

5 lbs baking potatoes

Wash and cube the potatoes. Cover them with water in a large pot and bring to a boil. Turn down the heat and simmer for about 20 minutes. You want them soft but not mushy.
Allow them to cool a little.

1 c vegetable broth (see stocks section)
2 tbsp soy sauce or tamari
4 tsp granulated garlic
1 c soy milk

In a food processor, put some of the cooked potatoes, about 1 1/2 cups, and one quarter each of the above four ingredients. Blend well, but not too long otherwise the potatoes will get sticky. Repeat the process four times until all the potatoes are puréed. Fill a baking dish with the potato soufflé and top with bread crumbs. Bake uncovered for 40 minutes at 375°.

# BROILED TAMARI TOFU

1/4 c soy sauce
1/4 c water
1 tsp granulated garlic
1/4 c chopped scallions
1 lb extra firm tofu

Combine the first four ingredients in a bowl. Cut a 1 pound package of Extra Firm Tofu into strips (approx. 3 inches long, 1/2 inch wide, and 1/4 inch thick).

Dredge the slices in the soy marinade for a minute or two, coating all the tofu slices. Place the tofu on a cookie sheet, and broil for 3 to 5 minutes.

Turn the slices over, and broil an additional 3 to 5 minutes. If you want them crispy, broil them longer. Watch carefully so they don't burn.

Serve hot.

Makes a great snack!

# DOLMADES
## (STUFFED GRAPE LEAVES)

The following is a basic recipe. You will find that you can be very creative and stuff the leaves with a variety of vegetables or grains. Some ideas follow.

Spread out the grapes leaves and cut off the little stem. Stack them in preparation for stuffing.

Filling for 20 leaves:

2C cooked basmati rice
1 1/2C water
1 small onion, chopped
1/2C celery chopped
1 garlic clove, minced
1/2C chopped tomatoes
1 tsp. basil leaves
1/2C cooked chic peas
1 tbs. soy sauce
1 1/2 tbs. cider vinegar
1 1/2 tbs. honey
2 tbs. capers (optional)

Prepare basmati rice and set aside. Combine next five ingredients, and simmer for 20 minutes.

*Continues...*

Drain off excess water and then transfer mixture to a bowl. Add all of the remaining ingredients, and combine well.

ASSEMBLE:

Lay 1 leaf out in front of you, veins facing up. Place 2 tbs. filling in center, near the bottom. Fold over the bottom and roll slightly, then turn in sides and continue to roll until closed. Line them up in a dish side by side. Sprinkle a little lemon juice over them and refrigerate until you are ready to serve them. You can serve these without sauce or with a little tomato sauce for dipping.

*Variations for Filling:*

*Brown rice, shredded carrots, onions, zucchini, and mushrooms.*
*Brown rice, chopped cashews with onions and mushrooms.*

# SESAME ASPARAGUS

1 1/2 tbs. olive oil
3/4C sliced leeks (washed well) or onions
2 cloves of garlic chopped
3 tbs. raw sesame seeds
1 1/2 lbs. asparagus

Sauté the first 3 ingredients for about 8 minutes and then add the sesame seeds. Lay the asparagus spears out along the bottom of the pan to cook. Move the onions around so the asparagus has enough room.

You don't want to overcook any ingredients in this dish; it cooks up very fast! After the spears are tender (3 - 4 minutes), pour 1 - 1 1/2 tbs. soy sauce on top. Stir well and turn off heat. Serve immediately.

## SESAME VEGETABLES

1-2 tbs. olive oil or canola oil
1/2C chopped onions
3 green onions, diced
2 cloves of garlic, minced
1C sliced mushrooms
1C sliced carrots
1C broccoli flowerettes
2C spinach leaves, washed and trimmed well
1/4C sesame seeds
1 tbs. soy sauce

Sauté the first four ingredients until the onions are translucent. Add the mushrooms, and cook for another 2 minutes. Add the other ingredients except the soy sauce. Toss well and cook for 6 more minutes. Add soy sauce and stir well.

Turn off heat.
Serve hot over rice or noodles or as a side dish.

# SWEET AND SOUR CABBAGE
*Serves 4.*

This dish is wonderfully tasty when served with brown rice and vegetable burgers.

1 tbs. olive oil
1C sliced onions
1 garlic clove, minced
1/2C green onion, chopped
6C sliced cabbage
5 Italian plum tomatoes, sliced into circles
2 1/2 tbs. wine vinegar
1 tsp. soy sauce
dash of pepper
2 tbs. honey

Sauté the first four ingredients until onions are translucent. Add cabbage, and cook for 5 minutes. Add tomatoes and the rest of the ingredients, and cook for about 8 more minutes.
Serve hot.

## AVOCADO AND RICE SUSHI
*Makes 8 rolls.*

To make the sushi rolls, purchase a rolling mat from your local health food store or local oriental store.

2C cooked brown rice
1/4C rice wine vinegar
2 tbs. honey
1 tbs. soy sauce or tamari
4 green onions, cleaned and split lengthwise
8 strips of carrots, about 6" long
16 slices of avocado
16 strips of tofu, about 3" long, 1/4" wide, 1/4" thick
8 rolls of Nori Seaweed

Combine the cooked rice with the next three ingredients, and set aside. Have the vegetables and tofu ready.

To assemble: Lay the mat in from of you, and place a piece of Nori seaweed on it. Pat rice about 1/8" thick from the bottom to almost the top, leaving about 1" empty.

Lengthwise place:

1 green onion
1 carrot
2 slices of avocado, end to end
2 strips of tofu, end to end

Carefully roll up from the bottom using the mat for support. When you get the to the top, gently wet the length of the Nori and it will seal the roll together as you roll it up.

Cut pieces crosswise about 1" thick. Stand each roll on end so you can see the vegetables. Any variety of vegetables works for the filling. Some might need a little blanching like asparagus or broccoli. Experiment. Enjoy.

Serve with Japanese horseradish and soy sauce.

## BABA GANOUJ
### (Middle Eastern Eggplant Spread)

2 1/2 lbs. of eggplant, whole

Skewer eggplants and roast them directly on a flame until they are charred thoroughly. Cool the eggplants and then scoop out the insides into a bowl. Mash the pulp, and combine it with the following:

4 - 6 tbs. lemon juice
1/4 C tahini
3 garlic cloves, minced
1/4 C chopped onion
1 tbs. tamari
3 springs of parsley, chopped well

Use as a dip for toasted breads, as a spread in a pita which has been stuffed with lots of vegetables, or as part of an antipasto.

# CORN AND BEAN NACHOS

2 large bags of water-baked no-oil tortilla chips
3 C refried beans (see page 194)
4 C cooked corn kernels
1/2 C shredded carrots
1 1/ 2 C grated soy cheese
2 C guacamole (see page 146)
1 C salsa (see page 145)

Preheat oven to 350°

Have all of the ingredients ready. Line a baking
dish with half of the tortillas. Layer the refried beans
on top and then the corn kernels. Spread out the
carrots and sprinkle with soy cheese.

Surround the nachos with the remaining chips
and bake at 350° for 20 minutes. Remove from oven
and garnish with guacamole and salsa.

## ROOT VEGETABLES WITH WHITE SAUCE

2 med size turnips, peeled and cut into 1/2" cubes
6 med. size leeks, white only, cut in 1/2" round pieces
   and washed well
1 C pearl onions, peeled
3 baking potatoes, cut into 1" chunks
2 1/2 C celery root, peeled and cut into 1/2" cubes

Place all vegetables in a pot and cover with cold water. Bring to a boil. Then, reduce heat and simmer for about 30 minutes until the vegetables are tender. Drain off all water and purée warm vegetables in a food processor.

Meanwhile, prepare white sauce:

2 C soy milk
4 tbsp whole wheat flour
1 tsp soy sauce
1/2 tsp granulated garlic
1 tbsp cooking sherry

Heat milk and whisk in flour. As sauce thickens slowly add the remaining ingredients. Pour over cooked root vegetable purée. Garnish with toasted sesame seeds.

# SWEET SWEET POTATOES

3 medium size sweet potatoes
2 cored green apples
dash of cumin
dash of cardamon
dash of cinnamon

Preheat oven to 450°

Bake potatoes for 15 minutes on a cooking sheet. Then add the cored apple. Continue baking for a about a half hour more. Remove the tough ends of the potatoes. Purée the apples and potatoes and spices in a food processor. Serve warm.

This dish can be made ahead of time and reheated in the oven or microwave.

# ENTRÉES

# STEWED VEGETABLES

1C purified water with a dash of soy sauce
2 medium size potatoes, sliced 1/8" thick, with skin on
(spread out slices)
1 large onion sliced, thinly and also spread out
2 sweet potatoes, thinly sliced and spread out
1C chopped broccoli
1C chopped cauliflower
1C corn kernels
1C green beans
2C sliced zucchini (or your favorite squash)
2 large tomatoes, sliced 1/4" thick and spread out
1 tsp. oregano
1 tsp. granulated garlic
1 1/2C water or vegetable stock

Be sure all vegetables are washed well. In a
heavy 6 qt. pot with a lid, layer the vegetables in the
order above.

Sprinkle top with oregano and garlic.

Cover and steam for 30 minutes. Serve with
rice or pasta or beans and pour some liquid on top.
*Continues...*

## VARIATIONS:

*Use green or red peppers, celery, peas, carrots.*

*Eggplants and mushrooms don't steam well, but mushroom stock can be substituted for water or vegetable stock.*

*Also, I love the taste of tomatoes with onions and potatoes. Sometimes I layer the tomato slices several times with herbs on top of them.*

*Beets will color your stew a beautiful pink.*

## STIR-FRY VEGETABLES WITH BROWN RICE

2 c short grain brown rice
4 1/2 c cold water

In a saucepan, combine the rice and water. Bring to a boil. Turn down heat to simmer and then cover, cooking for 35 minutes. Turn off heat. Leave lid on and allow rice to stand for 20 minutes.

Meanwhile, prepare Stir-Fry.

2 tbsp olive oil
2 med size onions, chopped
2 cloves of garlic, chopped
1 inch piece of ginger, sliced lengthwise
3 carrots, cut into diagonal slices 1/8 inch thick
2 c chopped celery
1 c sliced mushrooms
1 small green pepper, sliced
1 small red pepper sliced
1 1/2 c sliced zucchini or yellow squash
1 c broccoli flowerettes*
1 to 2 tbsp soy sauce or tamari (Japanese soy sauce)

*Continues...*

In a wok or skillet, heat the oil and add the next three ingredients. Stir and saute for 5 minutes. Next, add all remaining ingredients except for the soy sauce. Stir and cook for 8 more minutes. Add the soy sauce and stir all vegetables to coat them. Cook for another 2 to 3 minutes. Serve hot over a bed of short grain brown rice. Top with toasted sesame seeds.

*Green flower-like sections at the top of the stalk.

## STIR FRY WITH TOFU

Heat a wok or skillet for a minute or two.  Add:

1 tbsp sesame oil
1 tbsp soy oil
2 cut up onions
2 julienned carrots
a 2 inch slice of ginger, cut lengthwise
3 cloves of garlic, minced
1/2 c green onions, chopped

Sauté for 8 minutes, and then add:

1 c sliced mushrooms
1 1/2 c firm tofu, diced
2 oz prepared black mushrooms*
1 can sliced water chestnuts
1 head of bok choy , washed well & sliced

Sauté for another 5 minutes, and add:

2 c mung bean sprouts
1 to 2 tbsp soy sauce
1/4 c dry sherry or rice wine

Simmer for 3 minutes more, and serve hot on a
bed of short grain brown rice.

* Soak black mushrooms in 1 1/2C water for 1/2
hour.  When soft, cut off stems and slice the mushrooms lengthwise.

# SOUP-STEW

This can serve as a basic recipe for either a thick soup or a stew. You can vary it to add diversity to your menu and to accommodate what's in your refrigerator on any given day. I always make more than I need and freeze some. When put through a blender, it can become a sauce or a dip for chips.

Here are the basics:

3 onions, chopped
6 carrots, diced
1 bunch of celery, chopped (include leaves)
1 c chopped potato, unpeeled
1 parsnip, whole
2 tomatoes, chopped
4 cloves of garlic, chopped
2 tbsp soy sauce
2 tbsp sherry
2 zucchini, cut in 1/2 inch pieces
2 yellow squash, cut in 1/2 inch pieces
1 c cauliflower, chopped
1/2 c green pepper, chopped
1/2 c red pepper, chopped
1 bay leaf
1/2 bunch parsley
fresh dill or 2 tbsp dried dill weed
enough water to cover all vegetables and then some

Simmer all of the above ingredients for 1 1/2 hours. Remove the parsnip and the bunch of parsley. Serve hot with a big piece of bread.

# SWEET AND SOUR CHINESE VEGETABLES

1 tbs. sesame oil
1 tbs. canola oil
2C sliced onion
3 cloves of garlic, minced
1/2C chopped green onions
1" piece of ginger, sliced lengthwise in half
1C small button mushrooms
2C carrots, sliced diagonally in 1/4" thick pieces
1 1/2C celery, cut into 1" pieces
1C cauliflower flowerettes
1C snow peas
2C shredded Chinese cabbage
1C sliced tomatoes
1 1/2C mushroom stock (see page 63)
2C sweet and sour sauce (see page 72)

Sauté first six ingredients until the onions are translucent. Stir occasionally. Add the mushrooms and sauté for 3 minutes. Add each ingredient, one at a time, and stir well to combine. Add the stock. Mix well. Add the sweet and sour sauce. Turn down the heat so as not to burn the sauce.

Serve over rice garnished with chopped nuts.

# CURRIED VEGETABLES

2C cooked basmati rice
2 zucchinis, cubed into 1/2" chunks
1 yellow squash, cubed
1 carrot, grated
2 stalks of celery, chopped
1C peas
1C corn kernels
1 tsp. canola oil
1 onion, minced
2 garlic cloves, minced
3 1/2C butternut squash soup (see page 97)
1 - 2 tbs. curry paste
2 tbs. honey
1/2C apple juice
1/4C chopped parsley or cilantro

Prepare basmati rice (see grain chart), and set aside. Prepare all vegetables (except onions and garlic) and toss together in a bowl. Set aside.

In the canola oil, sauté the onions and garlic until the onions are translucent. Add the other vegetables and 1/2C water. Stir and cover to cook for 6 - 8 minutes, uncovered.

Combine the butternut squash soup, curry paste, and honey. Stir well and add to vegetables. Add the apple juice. Cover and simmer for 10 minutes. Add the parsley or cilantro. Stir well.

Serve hot over basmati rice and garnish with chopped nuts.

# MOROCCAN VEGETABLE GUMBO
## *Serves 4.*

1 1/2C cooked red beans  (see chart page 16 )
3 onions, sliced
4 cloves garlic, minced
1C chopped celery
1 1/2C diced carrots
3C diced sweet potatoes
1C diced zucchini
1/2C sliced red pepper
1 1/2c cubed tomatoes
3C vegetable stock
1C tomato juice or sauce
1 tbs. each, cumin, coriander and tumeric
1/2 tsp. cinnamon
1 tsp. soy sauce
dash each, cayenne, paprika, and saffron
2 tbs. honey
1/2C raisins

      Combine all of the ingredients except for raisins.
Make sure liquid reaches 3/4 of the way to the top of the
vegetables. (While cooking, the vegetables will make more
liquid.) Simmer for 25 minutes covered. Add raisins.
Continue cooking for 10 more minues, add beans. If you
need more liquid, add more stock. Adjust seasoning. Serve
warm with rice.

# SWEET POTATO PANCAKES
# WITH APPLE SAUCE

*Makes 10 to 18 pancakes.*

3 large sweet potatoes or yams
1/2 onion, grated
1/3 c whole wheat flour
1 egg white or egg replacer equivalent

Grate the potatoes and onions into a bowl. Add the flour and egg white, and combine. Batter should be firm enough to hold shape but not dry. If it is too wet, add a little more flour as needed. Use a non-stick griddle so you don't need oil. Form pancakes and heat until almost done. Turn pancakes over to brown other side.

## APPLESAUCE

3 sweet apples, cut into small pieces
1/2 c water or apple juice
1/2 tsp. cinnamon

Heat in a saucepan for about 10 minutes and serve warm with pancakes.

# STUFFED ZUCCHINI

*Serves 4.*
*(About 2 boats each)*

4 - 6" long zucchinis
2 tbs. olive oil
1/2C chopped green onion
1/2C chopped onion
1/2C chopped celery
3 cloves of garlic, minced
1 1/2C sliced mushrooms
1 tbs. soy sauce
1/2C bread crumbs
1/2 tsp. dried dill weed
dash of cayenne
paprika

Wash zucchinis and slice in half lengthwise. Cut out pulp, chop and reserve.

In a wok, heat the oil, and add the next four ingredients. Sauté until the onions are translucent, and add the mushrooms. Stir well and sauté for another 3 minutes.

Add the zucchini pulp and combine well. Season with the soy sauce. Remove to a bowl, and add all the remaining ingredients, except paprika. Fill the zucchini boats with the mushroom mixture, and top with a dash of paprika. Bake for 25 minutes at 350°.

Serve warm. A soy white sauce served with the zucchini is a nice addition, (see page 66).

# STUFFED ARTICHOKES

Take 4 firm, bright green artichokes. Trim the sharp points off the tips of the leaves and cut off the stems so the chokes can sit up.

Bring a large pot of water to a boil. (Artichokes like room to move.) Add 1/4 c lemon juice or squeeze in juice of 2 fresh lemons. This keeps the chokes from turning dark while they cook. Boil the artichokes for 35 minutes. You do not want to overcook them. Take a table knife and gently stab one through the bottom. If it is easy to do, then they are ready.

Remove the artichokes carefully, turning them upside down to drain and cool.

In the meantime, prepare the filling. Put 1 tbs. olive oil in a frying pan, and add:

1/2 c chopped green onions
1/2 c chopped celery
4 cloves of garlic, minced

Sauté for 5 minutes. Then add:

1 1/2 cups sliced mushrooms
1 c firm tofu, cut into small cubes
1 tbsp soy sauce                    *Continues...*

Cook for 3 to 4 more minutes and remove from heat.

Add:
3/4 c bread crumbs

Toss until well mixed.

Now back to the artichokes. Carefully open the top of each choke so you can get down to the center and remove the prickly leaves that surround the heart. I use a grapefruit spoon to scrape them out, being careful not to disturb the tender heart meat. When the inside of the choke is empty, add enough filling to come to the top and then sit the choke in a baking dish. Repeat with the other chokes and then bake at 350° for 15 minutes. No longer – you don't want them to dry out!

Now serve. (I open up the artichoke and eat some leaf and some filling at the same time. That way, I don't miss the taste of oily sauces!)

# SHISH KEBAB WITH TOFU ON BASMATI RICE

Prepare Basmati rice. (See chart page 15.)

2 tbsp soy sauce
1/4 c dry sherry
4 cloves of garlic, pressed or minced
3 green onions, chopped finely
1/4 c peanut sauce or honey
1/2 c purified water
2 c extra firm tofu, cubed into 1 inch cubes
    (large enough to run a skewer through them)

In a bowl, stir together all the ingredients except the tofu. When combined well, gently toss the tofu, and let it sit in the marinade while you prepare the other vegetables.

1 red pepper, cut into wide strips
1 green pepper, cut into wide strips
2 carrots, cut into rounds 1/4 inch thick
1 c pearl onions
1 lb button mushrooms
1 1/2 c cherry tomatoes

Remove tofu from marinade with a slotted spoon, and place in a bowl. Toss all the other vegetables gently in the marinade.

Take skewers or sticks and spear vegetables and tofu in a colorful order. For instance, try onion, tofu, tomato, green pepper, carrot, green pepper, tofu, and a mushroom. Place all the spears into a baking dish, and pour the marinade over them. Turn the skewers several times to wet all of the vegetables.

Barbecue the skewers, grill them on a home grill, or broil them in the oven until brown and cooked.

Serve on Basmati Rice. For a dipping sauce, you can select one of the sauces in the front section of this book.

# TOFU CHILI

*Serves 4.*

1 onion, chopped
2 cloves of garlic, chopped
1/2C celery
1/2C grated carrots
3 tbs. chopped green chilies
2C stewed tomatoes
3C fresh chopped tomatoes
1/2C chopped green pepper
1C vegetable broth
1C mashed tofu
2C cooked pinto beans
1C cooked kidney beans
1C garbanzo beans
1 1/2 tsp. chili powder
2 tbs. cumin
1 tsp soy sauce

Combine the first nine ingredients in a pot and bring to a boil. Turn down heat, and simmer for 20 minutes. Add all remaining ingredients and simmer for 35 minutes.

Serve with rice. For a spicy chili add a dash or two of Tabasco®.

# BARBECUED TOFU

2 cups short grain brown rice, cooked
1 lb. hard tofu, cut into strips 3" x 1" x 1/4" thick
1/2C water
2 tbs. soy sauce
2 tbs. red wine vinegar
1 tsp. granulated garlic
1/2C tomato sauce
1/4C water
2 tbs. honey
1 tbs. molasses
1/4C chopped onions
2 cloves of garlic, minced
1 tbs. vinegar
dash of soy sauce

Marinate tofu strips in the next four ingredients.

Combine tomato sauce and all remaining ingredients in a saucepan. Simmer until honey is dissolved. Lightly broil the tofu strips and then line them up in a baking dish. Pour the sauce on top. Broil for a few minutes until brown.

Serve on a bed of brown rice.

# BURRITOS WITH REFRIED BEANS

## REFRIED BEANS

Cover 2 c dried pinto or black beans with purified water, and soak them overnight in a cool place. In the morning, drain the water. Cover the beans with fresh water, and cook for 1 1/2 hours until they are soft. Drain beans, and save liquid for use in soups. This stock can be frozen in easy-to-thaw-and-use portions.

2 tbsp. molasses
1/4 c honey
1/2 c tomato sauce
 cooked beans

In a saucepan, combine all the ingredients, including cooked beans. Heat, stirring constantly. If the beans begin sticking to the pan, scrape the bottom with a wooden spoon.*

When the beans are soft and the liquid has turned "saucy" (in about 8 to 10 minutes), remove from heat.

## RICE

2 c cooked short grain brown rice.

Prepare rice. (See grain chart on page 15).

*Continues...*

## FILLING

1 tbsp soy oil
1 large onion, sliced thinly
2 carrots, cut into thin 2 inch strips or grated
4 stalks of celery cut into thin 2 inch strips
2 cloves of garlic, chopped
1 c tomato wedges
1/2 c red and green pepper slices (combined)
2 c zucchini or yellow squash or broccoli or mush
rooms, all cut into thin strips
2 tbsp soy sauce or tamari
1c grated soy cheese

Heat oil in a wok or frying pan, and saute´ the onions until they are translucent. Then add all of the other vegetables and saute´ for 8 minutes. Add the soy sauce, mix well, and then turn off heat.

To assemble burritos:

Place a tortilla in your hand, and spread 3 tbsp of refried beans on tortilla. Add 1/4 to 1/3 c vegetables, top with rice, and fold over the tortilla. Place the finished tortilla in a rectangular Pyrex® baking dish. Continue filling the tortillas and placing them in the dish until you run out of vegetables. Top with grated soy cheese. Bake at 350° only for 10 minutes. You want the cheese to melt without the burritos drying out.
Serve with Salsa and Guacamole. (See recipes in the Aside section.)

*(Metal utensils may scratch the bottom of a no-stick pan. Use wooden utensils for cooking whenever possible.)

# SAUTÉED LEEKS

Prepare 2c cooked short grain brown rice or make Basmati rice which is an Indian white or brown grain with a nutty flavor. (See grain chart on page 15.)

## SAUTÉED LEEKS

2 tbsp olive oil
4 leeks, washed & chopped
   (use white parts only)
1 onions, chopped
1 clove garlic, chopped
1 yellow pepper, sliced thinly
1 c of sliced mushrooms
1 lb broccoli flowerets or asparagus spears
1 tbsp soy sauce
2 tbsp sherry
1 tbsp raw sesame seeds

*Continues...*

Heat the oil and sauté the next three ingredients until the onions are translucent. Add the next three ingredients and sauté for 5 more minutes. Add the soy sauce and sherry, and combine all of the vegetables well. Cook for 3 more minutes.

Serve hot over a bed of rice and top with sesame seeds.

## CUBAN-CHINESE RICE & BEANS

Many years ago, I shared a summer house with a lady named Carmen. One day as I was preparing a Chinese meal for about 12 people, Carmen came into the kitchen and said she would like to make Cuban rice and have Cuban-Chinese food for dinner! What an odd combination I thought, never realizing the history of such a combination would be so interesting. Many Chinese people were the laborers on the railway system in South and Central America so many Chinese cooking techniques were used with local produce. I'm sure that the new ingredients of the region such as peppers, olives, and tomatoes were tasty. They slowly became a part of the diet mixed with oriental spices, rices, and other exotic dishes. So here is what Carmen and I cooked:

2C cooked black beans
3C  cooked short grain brown rice
1 tbs. olive oil
1 onion, chopped
2 cloves of garlic, chopped
1 jalapeno pepper, chopped (If you like spicy food, do
    not take out  the seeds. If you like mild tastes,
remove the seeds.  Wear gloves, and wash your hand,
and don't touch your face!)

1/2C chopped, green onions
1/4C chopped cilantro
1C chopped tomatoes
1/4C chopped black olives
1/4C chopped green pepper
1 tsp. cumin
1 tsp. paprika
1 tbs. soy sauce
2C mung beans sprouts

Prepare beans.  Prepare rice.

Sauté onion, garlic, pepper and green onions in olive oil until onions are translucent.  Add the remaining ingredients and combine well.  Add the cooked black beans.

Cook for 5 more minutes.  Toss with the cooked brown rice and serve hot.

# RICE WITH RAISINS AND NUTS

4C cooked basmati rice, short grain brown rice, or wild rice
2C vegetable broth
1C chopped leeks
1/2C chopped green onion
juice from 3 cloves of garlic
1 tbs. soy sauce
1/2 C chopped celery
1C chopped broccoli
1 tbs. cumin
1 tbs. dried dill weed
1/2C raisins
1C mung bean sprouts
1/4C almonds
1/4C pine nuts
1/4C cashews
1/4C parsley

Prepare rice and set aside. Combine the next seven ingredients in a saucepan. Cook for 10 minutes, and add the next four ingredients. Continue simmering for 10 more minutes. Add the rice, and simmer for 5 more minutes.

Purée the nuts and parsley in the blender to a coarse meal.

Serve the rice and vegetables hot with nut parsley garnish on top.

# VEGETABLES RISOTTO

*Serves 4.*

9C vegetable stock
1 tbs. soy sauce
1 tbs. olive oil
3/4C minced onion
1/4C green onion, finely chopped
3 cloves of garlic, minced
2C long grain brown rice (uncooked)
1C chopped mushrooms
1 1/2C sherry
1/4C fresh, shelled peas
1/2C small broccoli flowerettes
1/2C yellow squash, chopped into small pieces
1/4C minced parsley

Bring vegetable stock and soy sauce to a boil. Lower heat, and keep on simmer. Meanwhile, heat oil and add onions, green onions, and garlic. Sauté for 5 minutes and then add the rice. Stir until all of the ingredients are mixed, and add the mushrooms. Stir and cook for 3 more minutes.

*Continues...*

Add 2 cups of vegetable broth, and allow it to cook out until no liquid is left. Add the sherry, the vegetables, and 2 tbs. of parsley. Add 2 more cups of stock, and simmer until the liquid cooks out. Add the remaining stock. Continue cooking until only a little bit of stock is left (30 minutes or so). The rice should be soft and the vegetables tender. Garnish with the remaining parsley.

# PASTA WITH TOMATO SAUCE

Choose an interesting pasta so the kids will enjoy the meal. Now let's make a healthy sauce.

2 carrots, chopped
4 stalks of celery , chopped
1 onion, sliced

Cover the ingredients with purified water, and bring to a boil. Simmer for 15 minutes. Remove from the heat, and cool slightly. Drain the vegetables, reserving the liquid, and purée in the blender. (You can save the liquid, freeze it, and add it to soup later.) If you have tomato sauce made, just add the vegetable purée. If you need to make tomato sauce, here's a basic recipe.

4 lbs Italian plum tomatoes, chopped
1 large can tomato paste
1/2 c purified water
1 tbsp basil leaves
1 bay leaf
1/2 tbsp oregano
1 tsp granulated garlic                    *Continues...*

Combine all ingredients and simmer for 1 hour. Stirring occasionally so the sauce doesn't stick to the pot. Keep the heat low. When the sauce is done, you can add the vegetable purée mixture. Serve over pasta.

(Note: This is a great way to get more vitamins and minerals into the kids, and this dish tastes terrific!)

# JAPANESE PASTA WITH JULIENNED VEGETABLES

Buy soba noodles, which are available in most markets and health food stores in the oriental food section. They have a subtle taste and make a nice change from more familiar pastas. Cook according to directions on package.

To julienne vegetables, cut them in long, thin strips about 2 1/2 inches long.

1 tsp sesame oil
1 tbsp soy oil
1 1/2 c sliced onions
1/2 c green onions
2 cloves garlic, minced
1 1/2 c julienned carrots
1 1/2 c julienned celery
1 c sliced mushrooms
1 c red or green (or mixed) julienned peppers
1 c broccoli flowerettes
1 1/2 tbsp soy sauce
dash of cayenne
1/4 c peanut sauce*
1/2 c water

*Continues...*

Heat oil and sauté the next three ingredients for 8 minutes. Then add the carrots and celery and sauté for three more minutes. Add the remaining vegetables. Toss well and continue cooking. Then add the soy sauce, cayenne, peanut sauce, and water. Stir well. Cook for five more minutes and remove from heat.

Portion out noodles on plates, and top with vegetables. Toasted sesame seeds are a tasty garnish.

*Can be purchased in health food stores.

## "PORK" AND BEANS

In the health food stores, and now in many supermarkets, you can find an assortment of soy "hot dogs."

Try several brands, and choose your family's favorite for this dish.

Split the franks lengthwise and place them on the grill or griddle to cook. Heat until they are cooked through – about 10 minutes. Set aside.

Prepare red kidney beans. (See chart page 16). In a frying pan add:

3C beans, cooked
1 onion, chopped
1 clove of garlic, minced
1 tomato, chopped

Cook over low heat, scraping the bottom of the pan so the beans don't stick.

Cut the franks into 1 inch pieces and add to bean mixture.

Serve hot.

# STUFFED CABBAGE

1 large cabbage
3C cooked brown rice
1 tbs. olive oil
1 onion, chopped
2 cloves of garlic, minced
1C chopped celery
1C chopped carrots
1C grated zucchini
1/4C chopped red or green pepper (optional)
1C sliced mushrooms
1 tbs. tamari
1/2C raisins

## SAUCE:

1 large can chopped tomatoes
8 oz. can tomato purée
2 tbs. vinegar
2 tbs. honey

Steam cabbage for 15 minutes. Drain water.
Cool. Prepare rice (see chart page 15). Sauté next
five ingredients until onion is translucent, then add
the next three ingredients. Sauté for 6 minutes more.
Add tamari and raisins. Toss well. Remove
from heat. In a bowl, combine cooked rice and vegetables.
*Continues...*

Set aside. Combine sauce ingredients, and mix well. Heat them until the honey dissolves.

TO ASSEMBLE:

Peel away, carefully, all the cabbage leaves. Cut out the hard core and stem, leaving as much of the leaves intact as possible. Lay a leaf out flat, outside down, and fill with 4 - 6 tbs. of rice filling. Roll up, starting from the bottom and folding in the sides.

Place all the rolled cabbage in a baking dish side by side. Pour tomato sauce on top, and bake covered for 1hour and 15 minutes at 375°. Uncover and bake for 20 minutes more.

Serve hot.

## POLENTA AND SQUASH

2C corn meal
6C water
1 butternut squash
1/2 lb. tofu, cubed
1 tbs. olive oil
1 onion, chopped
2 garlic cloves, chopped
1C chopped carrots
1C chopped celery
2C chopped Italian plum tomatoes
1 1/2C vegetable broth
1 tbs. soy sauce
1C green beans
1C cauliflower, cut into pieces
1 tbs. cumin

Prepare Polenta by bringing the water to a boil and slowly pouring in the corn meal while constantly stirring.

Simmer for about 15 minutes, stirring all the while. When thick, pour into a lightly greased 12" x 12" casserole dish and allow to cool. After an hour, you can refrigerate it.

*Continues...*

Cut off the outer skin of the butternut squash, and discard the seeds and "threads" from the inside. Dice the "meat" into small cube shapes. Simmer the cubes for 8 minutes until tender. When slightly cooled, blend the squash into a smooth purée. Set aside.

Cut tofu into 1/2" cubes, and set aside. In a wok, heat the oil and add the onion and garlic.

Sauté for 5 minutes, and add the tofu. Continue cooking and moving the ingredients around with a wooden spoon. After 4 minutes, add the carrots and celery. Combine well and then add the tomatoes, broth, cooked squash, green beans, cauliflower, and cumin. Simmer for 10 - 15 minutes more.

While the vegetables continue to cook, take out the Polenta and cut into 1" cubes. Have ready about 3 - 4 cupfuls. When the vegetables are done, toss in the polenta cubes only for a minute to heat up.

Serve this dish warm garnished with chopped parsley.

# SOY CHEESE PIZZA

You can buy pizza dough or pizza pie shells, but here's my recipe. Then add your own vegetable tomato sauce (see recipe on page 203), the kids' favorite vegetables, and top with grated soy cheese. Bake until the cheese is browned.

### Pizza Dough Recipe:

1 pkg dry yeast
1 1/3 c warm (not hot) water
pinch of sugar
2 tbsp olive oil
dash of salt
2 c sifted flour
1 c whole wheat flour

Combine the yeast, water, and pinch of sugar in a bowl. Cover and let stand in a warm place (the inside of an unlit gas oven is usually 85°).

Sift the flours together. When the yeast rises, add the rest of the ingredients and yeast mix to the flours. Knead for about 10 minutes, and let rise once, covered in a warm place for about 2 hours.

*Continues...*

Lightly oil 2 pizza pie pans 12 inch diameter or a cookie sheet. When the dough is ready, put it down and stretch it out to fill the pans.

Pinch up the edges to form a little wall to hold the sauce and vegetables. Prick the dough with a fork several times.

Spread sauce and vegetables and top with grated soy cheese.

Bake at 400° for about 1/2 hour.

## LASAGNA WITH WHITE SAUCE AND CORN

2C grated soy cheese
4C unflavored soy milk
1C whole wheat flour
12 - 16 strips of lasagna
1 1/2 tbs. olive oil
3 onions, chopped
4 garlic cloves, minced
2C chopped celery
3C sliced mushrooms
4C cooked corn kernels
1 tbs. soy sauce
1 tbs. dry dill weed
1 tbs. dry basil leaves
1/2 tsp. ground white pepper

Prepare white sauce by bringing soy milk to a boil.

Turn down heat to simmer, slowly pouring in the flour while stirring. When the sauce thickens, turn off heat and set aside.

It is not necessary to cook the lasagna strips. They will soften when baked in the sauce. If you choose to cook them, keep them *al dente* (not soft).

In a skillet, heat the oil, onions, and garlic.

After 5 minutes, add the celery and mushrooms, and continue cooking and stirring with a wooden spoon for 6 more minutes. Add all the remaining ingredients, and cook for another 5 minutes. Turn off the heat and set aside.

TO ASSEMBLE:

Layer a few spoonfuls of white sauce on the bottom of a casserole dish. Now lay out 3 or 4 strips of lasagna.

Layer the vegetables and then the grated soy cheese. Spoon some white sauce on the top, and repeat ending with the remaining white sauce.

Bake at 375° covered for 1 hour and then remove cover. Continue baking for 20 minutes more.

# TOFU LASAGNA

*Serves 6 - 8.*

2 lbs. hard tofu
1 tbs. olive oil
3 onions, chopped
4 garlic cloves, minced
3C grated carrots
3C chopped celery
4C sliced mushrooms
3C chopped zucchini
3C chopped broccoli
3C chopped chard - green or red
5C tomato sauce
3C soy mozzarella cheese, grated

Prepare tofu by cutting 1/8" thick slices. Keep the length the size of the 1 pound block. Each piece should be about 4 1/2" x 2 1/2" x 1/8" thick. You'll end up with about 20 pieces.

Heat oil in skillet, and add onions and garlic. After 5 minutes, add the carrots, celery, and mushrooms. Continue cooking (always mixing with a wooden spoon). After 5 more minutes, add the remaining vegetables. Cook for 5 more minutes. Remove vegetables to a bowl, and set aside.

*Continues...*

To Assemble:

In a 12" x 16" x 3" deep casserole (approximately), first spread 3/4C tomato sauce and then lay out 1/3 of the tofu end to end. Pour 1/2 the vegetable mix on top and spread it out.

Sprinkle 1C soy cheese evenly on top, and then pour on 1 1/2C tomato sauce and spread it evenly. Repeat, starting with the tofu, and then the vegetable mix, soy cheese, tofu, and tomato sauce.

Bake at 375° for 1 1/2 hours covered. Remove the cover, and then bake for 20 minutes more.

You can make this in two batches, by doubling the recipe. After they cool, you can wrap one well and freeze it. I always make more than one at a time, because it's a process. Later you can defrost one and bake it again when you have company or not much time to cook!

# SPINACH AND NUT PESTO

*Makes 4 cups.*

Pesto is traditionally a summer sauce in Italy where basil grows so profusely. Here are a few varieties on the basic theme. I have excluded most of the oil, which is abundant in the Italian Pesto. To make the sauce more moist, you can add chopped tomatoes or soy milk.

In a food processor, purée:

2C fresh basil
4C fresh spinach, washed well and firmly packed
1/2C lemon juice
1 tbs. olive oil
4 cloves of garlic, minced
1/2 C pine nuts
1/4C walnuts or hazelnuts *
1/2C washed parsley
1 tsp. soy sauce

Optional:

1/2 pound hard tofu
1/4C water
substitute chard for spinach (or just add some)

*Continues...*

Pestos are wonderful served with pastas, but also nice with short grain brown rice with pine nuts sprinkled on top.

\* Hazelnuts taste less bitter with the skins removed.  Bake in the oven on a cookie sheet for 15 minutes and then cool for 10 minutes.  Rub the nuts in a towel, and the skins will come off easily.

# STUFFED WONTONS
*Makes 30 wontons.*

Buy wonton skins at your local market. Read the labels carefully. Look for packaged wontons without additives.

Filling:
1 tsp sesame oil
1 tsp soy oil
1 to 2 inch piece of ginger, sliced lengthwise
1 onion, chopped
2 carrots, grated
1/2 c chopped celery
1 c grated mushrooms
1tbsp soy sauce
1/2 c bread crumbs

Heat oil in a wok or skillet and add the next four ingredients. Stir-fry for 6 minutes. Add the mushrooms and continue cooking for another 2 minutes, then add the soy sauce. Turn off heat and spoon vegetables into a bowl. Add the bread crumbs, and mix well. Set aside,and allow to cool for a half hour.

To assemble, have a small bowl of water handy. Lay out a wonton skin, and spoon 1 tsp of filling into the center. Dip a clean finger into the water, and wet 2 adjacent edges of the wonton skin. Fold the other 2 edges over to form a triangle shape, and press them together. Place on a baking sheet. You can do this assembly-line fashion, wetting each one just before you fold it over.

Set up a steamer. Lightly oil the basket, and steam wontons for 2 minutes. Serve with peanut sauce or soy sauce. These can be made the day before and sealed with plastic wrap in the refrigerator.

## CREPES

Crepes are incredibly versatile.

Use the soy pancake recipe (see page 22) and add 1/4C more soy milk. If these are dessert crepes, add 1/2 tsp. vanilla.

No egg or oil is necessary. (You can even buy soy milk which is low in fat.) Buy a crepe maker! It makes the process easy and fun, and usually they require no oil!! Experiment with size and shape.

Here are three FILLINGS and sauce suggestions:

## MUSHROOMS AND SPINACH CREPES WITH WHITE SAUCE

1 tbs. olive oil
1C chopped onion
2 cloves garlic, minced
2C sliced mushrooms
3C chopped spinach
1/2 tsp. thyme
1 tbs. soy sauce
2C White Sauce
   (see page 66) with a dash of nutmeg

Sauté the first three ingredients for 6 minutes. Add the mushrooms. Sauté for 3 more minutes, and add the spinach, thyme, soy sauce. Stir and set aside. Mix in 3 tbs. of white sauce. After filling each crepe with mushroom filling, pour a little soy white sauce on top!

## MEXICAN CREPES WITH TOMATO SAUCE

1 tbs. olive oil
1C chopped onions
2 cloves of garlic, minced
1/4C green pepper, chopped
1 small jalapeno pepper, seeded and chopped
1/2C diced mushrooms
1C chopped tomatoes
2C pinto beans, cooked
1/4C cilantro leaves, chopped or 2 tbs. dried cilantro
dash of Tabasco® (optional)
2C tomato sauce (see page 203)
1/4C cilantro leaves
1C grated soy cheese


Sauté the first five ingredients for 8 minutes. Add the next four ingredients and stir well. Add Tabasco® if desired. Cook for 8 minutes.

In a saucepan, combine tomato sauce and cilantro and then simmer. Fill each crepe with bean mixture. Roll them up, and top with some tomato sauce and grated soy cheese.

# ORIENTAL CREPES

1 tbs. sesame oil
1 tbs. soy oil
1C shredded onion
2 garlic cloves, minced
1" slice of ginger, cut into 4 pieces
1C chopped green onion
1C shredded carrots
2C shredded Chinese cabbage
2C mung bean sprouts
1 tbs. soy sauce
2 tbs. rice vinegar
1 tbs. honey
1 can Chinese straw mushrooms

Sauté the first six ingredients for 8 minutes. Add the next three ingredients, and combine well. Sauté for 3 minutes and then add the soy sauce, rice vinegar, and honey.

Stir well, and cook for 3 more minutes. Add the straw mushrooms (found in most supermarkets).

Remove from heat, and fill crepes. We like a peanut sauce diluted with water as a dipping sauce for the crepes.

## CREPE SOUBISE

This is a variation of one of my favorite French recipes. Prepare six crepes as in soy pancake recipe (see page 22) adding 1/4C more soy milk for each batch of six. Set aside.

3 C of soy milk
3/4C whole wheat flour
1 tbs. safflower oil
3C chopped onion
3 cloves of garlic, minced
1/4C chopped shallots
1 1/2C sliced mushrooms
1 tsp. soy sauce
1/2C sherry

Bring soy milk to a boil, and then turn down heat. Add whole wheat flour, and whisk until sauce is thick. Set aside.

Sauté the next three ingredients in the safflower oil for 4 minutes. Add the mushrooms and soy sauce, and cook for another 5 minutes. Set aside in a bowl.

In a saucepan, bring the sherry to a boil and reduce to 1/4C. Add this to the white sauce, and whisk well.

To assemble crepe soubise, layer a crepe, a fifth of the onion mixture, and then two spoonfuls of white sauce.

Repeat until a crepe is on top. Spoon the rest of the sauce over the crepes, and bake for 15 minutes at 350°. Serve hot.

# BRAISED VEGETABLES

1/2 C soy sauce
1/4 C water
1/4 C balsamic vinegar
2 tbsp olive oil
4 cloves of garlic, minced

Combine all of the ingredients for the marinade.

2 C broccoli flowers, slightly steamed
1 bunch baby carrots, no greens
1 C button mushrooms
1 C pearl onions, peeled and cut in half
1 eggplant, peeled and cut into 1/4" medallions
2 zucchini cut into 1/4" thick rounds
1 fennel bulb, quartered
2 leeks, washed well and cut into long strips

Prepare all vegetables and line them up single layer on a baking dish. Brush with marinade and broil until brown. Turn vegetable over to brown on all sides. Serve with rice.

# INDIAN PANCAKES (DOSAS)

2 C brown rice flour
1/2 C soy flour
2 C water
dash of salt

     Combine all ingredients and make pancakes, dropping 3 tbsp of batter on a hot griddle. Dosas are wonderful served warm and filled with Masala potatoes and dal. (See page 152).

### MASALA POTATOES

2 medium size baked potatoes
1 tbs olive oil
1 tsp mustard seeds
1/2 tsp cumin
1/2 tsp coriander
1 tbsp cilantro leaves
1 tbsp soy sauce
1 tbsp turmeric
1/2 C chopped onion
1 C vegetable broth

     Bake potatoes and allow to cool. When cooled, cut into 1" pieces.

Heat oil and add mustard seeds. When they begin to pop add all of the other spices. Combine well and add the chopped onion. Sauté for 5 minutes and then add the cooled pieces of potato. Add broth and simmer for 15 minutes, combining all ingredients well. Served stuffed into Dosas with dal.

Tomato relish is a wonderful complement to this dish. (See page 52.)

# SEITAN

# SEITAN

Once you have discovered wheat gluten, Seitan, you will either be won over or not. Seitan is an Oriental food made from a process of kneading the flour under water until only the chewy substance remains. It is rubbery and versatile. The taste of spare ribs, chili, meatballs, patties, and steak are just a few of the flavors you can duplicate with seasonings and processes.

Seitan is found in health food stores in the refrigerator or freezer. It is dated and should not be used after the expiration date. There are also different kinds of Seitan. Some are rubbery and come packaged in liquid. These are great for patties, meatballs, chicken, and veal flavor dishes. The hard or block shape Seitan is great for pepper steak, fajitas, spareribs, or sweet and sour dishes. I have included some of our favorites. Try not to be intimidated by this new product. Just dive in and you will see how easy and versatile it is.

# SEITAN WITH TOMATOES & GARLIC
### *Serves 4.*

1 lb. cake of Seitan, cut in 1" x 3" x 1/4" strips
1C water
2 tbs. soy sauce
2 tbs. balsamic vinegar
1 1/2 tbs. olive oil
4 cloves of garlic, chopped
1/2C chopped green onion
3C chopped Italian plum tomatoes
1 tsp. basil
dash of oregano
1 bay leaf
1/2 tsp. cumin
1/4C chopped parsley
2 dashes of Tabasco®

Combine water, soy sauce, and vinegar. Stir to combine and marinate the Seitan for 1 hour. Sauté the onions and garlic in oil until the onions are translucent. Now add the tomatoes and the remaining ingredients. Cook for 15 minutes. Add the seitan. (Save the marinade in a sealed jar in the refrigerator, and reuse within the week.)

Continue simmering for 1/2 hour. Serve over fettuccini.

# PEPPER STEAK

*Serves 4.*

1 1/2 tbs. olive oil
1 large onion, sliced
3 cloves of garlic, chopped
1C cut celery 1" long chunks
1 1/2C sliced carrots, 1/2" thick rounds
1 1/2C sliced mushrooms
1C cut bell pepper
 (green, yellow, red or some of each), long slices
1 lb. hard Seitan, cut into strips 1" x 1/4" x 2"
2 tbs. soy sauce

In a wok, heat the oil and sauté onion and garlic for 5 minutes. Add the next three ingredients, and continue cooking for 5 more minutes. Add the peppers, and stir well.

Now, one piece at a time, lay the Seitan strips on the bottom and sides of the wok pushing the vegetables aside. You want to brown the Seitan.

Continue until all pieces are in the wok and then start turning them over to brown the other side. When they are all brown, mix the Seitan and vegetables together. Add the soy sauce and 1C purified water. Simmer in the wok for 5 more minutes, and serve with brown rice.

# BARBECUE

*Serves 4.*

1 lb. Seitan
1C barbecue sauce (see page 76.)
1/2C water

Prepare Seitan by cutting it into strips 1" x 1/4" x 3" long. Mix together sauce and water, and marinate strips for a few hours. Now arrange them side by side on a cookie sheet, and either barbecue them or broil them.

Top with barbecue sauce, and serve with Polenta (see page 210).

# FAJITAS

*Serves 4.*

2 tbs. soy sauce
1/2 tsp. granulated garlic
1/4C balsamic vinegar
1/4C water
1/2 lb. Seitan, cut into thin long "shredded" strips
1 tsp. olive oil
1 onion, sliced thinly
2  green chilies, chopped
2 peppers, sliced thinly
2C chopped tomatoes

Combine the first four ingredients. Add the Seitan, and marinate for 3 - 4 hours. In a wok or skillet, heat the oil and add the onions, chilies, and peppers. Sauté for 8 minutes. Now add the tomatoes, and cook for another 5 minutes. Add the Seitan, and sauté for 5 - 10 minutes. Fill warm tortillas with the vegetable - Seitan mix, and roll them up.

Serve with guacamole or a spicy red chili sauce (see page 75).

This makes a fun lunch!

# MEATBALLS OR PATTIES

Toast 1/4C sesame seeds. Set aside.

Sauté in 1 tbs. olive oil for 8 minutes:

1/2 onion, minced
1 clove garlic, minced
1/2C grated mushrooms
1/2C grated carrots

In a food processor, place 1 pound wet Seitan with 1 - 2 tbs. liquid from the Seitan.

Add sautéed vegetables and sesame seeds, and turn off and on a few times until all is blended. Put mixture in a bowl, and add 2 - 4 tbs. unbleached flour. Mix well. The mixture should not be too wet. You want it to form balls or patties without falling apart. If it is too wet, add more flour slowly. Mix well. Form. Shape. For 'meat' balls, drop seitan balls into hot tomato sauce and cook for 30 minutes.

To form patties, preheat oven to 350°. Place patties on parchment paper on a cookie sheet. Bake 15 minutes on one side and then turn them over and bake for 10 minutes more.

Serve with ketchup or peanut sauce or in a bun with a slice of onion and tomato.

# STROGANOFF

1 1/2 tbs. olive oil
1 onion, chopped
1C chopped celery
3 cloves garlic, minced
1 1/2C button mushrooms, whole
1 1/2 tbs. soy sauce
1/4C wine or sherry
1 pound Seitan (a soft Seitan is best),
   cut up or sliced thin
1C vegetable broth
1C cooked black beans
1/2C sour cream substitute or non-fat plain yogurt

    In a saucepan, sauté the first four ingredients until the onions are translucent. Add the mushrooms, and stir well.

    Add the soy sauce and sherry. Allow a minute or two for the alcohol to boil out and then add the strips of Seitan. Cook for about 3 minutes, and add the stock and beans. Cover and simmer for about 8 minutes. Remove from the heat.

    Serve on noodles with a dollop of sour cream substitute or non-fat yogurt.

## STEW

2 onions, cut up
3 carrots, cubed
1 1/2C cut up celery
3 cloves of garlic, chopped
2 Idaho or russet potatoes, cubed
1 zucchini, sliced
2 tomatoes, cut up (skin and seeds are OK)
1 sweet potato, cut into 1" chunks
1 pound Seitan, cubed (1" cubes)
1 quart vegetable broth
1 tbs. soy sauce
1/4C chopped parsley
1/2 tsp. cayenne
1/2 tsp. thyme
1 tsp. cumin
green or red pepper (optional)

Combine all ingredients in a "stew" pot.

Bring to a boil, turn down flame, and simmer for 1 hour. When Seitan is tender (may be another 15 - 20 minutes), the stew is ready to serve. Serve over pasta or rice. To thicken sauce, dissolve 2 tbs. arrowroot in 1/4C water and pour slowly into stew.

NOTE: I sometimes make this the night before. It marinates well.

## MARSALA

1 lb. soft Seitan
1 1/2 tbs. olive oil
1C chopped onions
1/4C chopped shallots
3 cloves of garlic, minced
2C sliced mushrooms
1/2C Marsala wine
1C vegetable broth
2 tbs. parsley
1 tbs. soy sauce
1 tbs. corn starch
1/4C cold water

Cut Seitan in 2" x 1" x 1/4" pieces, and set aside. In a skillet, heat the oil and sauté the onions, shallots, and garlic for 5 minutes. Add the mushrooms and continue sautéing for 5 more minutes. Add the Marsala wine. Allow the alcohol to boil out (about 3 minutes). Pour in the stock, and add the parsley and soy sauce. Add the seitan pieces and continue cooking for 10 minutes.

Dissolve corn starch in water, and slowly add it to the sauce to thicken. Seitan Marsala tastes wonderful served over wild rice. Serve hot.

# BREADS

## BREAD

I'm only going to include one yeast bread recipe in this book because there are already wonderful bread-making books on the shelves. Baking is a very precise art, and the purpose of this book is to acquaint you with interesting uncomplicated recipes so that you can ease into a new way of eating. I have included several muffin and "quick" bread recipes. These are fun to make and easy enough for the kids to help.

# BRAN MUFFINS

*Makes 8 to 10 muffins.*

2 c unbleached flour
3 c bran
1 tsp baking powder
1 tsp soy oil
1 c soy milk
1/2 c apple juice
1 egg white (or an egg equivalent found in health food
    stores called Egg Replacer®)
1/4 c molasses
1/4 c brown sugar or honey
1/4 c raisins or 1/2 c seasonal fruit
    (Peaches, strawberries and blueberries are great!)

Preheat oven to 350° Combine first three ingredients in a bowl and set aside. Combine all other ingredients and mix thoroughly. Add the dry ingredients to the wet ingredients and combine well, but do not beat.

Line a muffin tin with paper cupcake liners and pour the batter evenly in each liner. Bake for 18 to 20 minutes (a little longer if they are still wet). Let stand for 5 minutes and then remove the muffins to a wire rack to cool.

You can prepare the batter the night before and refrigerate it, but don't add the fruit until just before baking.

Let the refrigerated batter stand at room temperature for a 1/2 hour before baking.

## RAISIN BRAN BREAD

*Makes 1 loaf*

Preheat oven to 350°.  In a bowl combine:

1C whole wheat flour
1C all purpose flour
1/4C wheat germ
1 1/2C bran
3 tbs. baking powder
1 tsp. cinnamon

In another bowl combine:

1/3C Egg Beaters®
1/4C honey
2 tbs. molasses
1 tbs. olive oil
1/2C raisins

Mix all wet ingredients well and then add dry ingredients.  Oil a 5" x 9" loaf pan.  Form loaf shape, and place in pan.  Allow 1 hour to rise and then bake at 350° for an hour.  Test to make sure bread is done by sticking a toothpick in it.  It should come out "clean."

*Continues...*

If it still feels wet, you may need to bake it for another 10 minutes. Allow to cool on a rack before removing from loaf pan.

This is a "thick" bread, unlike "fluffy" sandwich bread. We snack on this bread. I love it toasted.

## ZUCCHINI WHEAT BREAD
*Makes 1 loaf*

This is a dense bread which toasts up wonderfully, and it is quite tasty eaten as a snack plain with no toppings or spreads. I love to serve this bread hot with soup in the winter.

In a sauce pan, scald.

2/3C soy milk

Remove from heat and add:

1 tbs. olive oil
2 tbs. brown sugar
2 tbs. applesauce

Stir well until sugar is melted.

In a bowl combine:

1 1/2C whole wheat flour
1 1/2C all purpose flour
1/4C wheat germ
1 tsp. ground cardamom

*Continues...*

249

Stir with a wooden spoon, and add the liquid mixture.

Add:

1 1/2C shredded zucchini
3/4C raisins (optional)

Knead for 10 minutes. The batter will be slightly moist. In a warm place, let rise in an oiled bowl for 1 1/2 hours covered.

Punch down. Knead for 10 minutes, shape into a loaf, and put in an oiled loaf pan.

Allow to rise one more hour and then bake at 350° for approximately 40 minutes.

It can be slightly moist inside,  but not wet! After it cools, slice it and serve.

# ZUCCHINI MUFFINS

*8 muffins*

Preheat oven to 375°. Line muffin tin with paper liners.

Sift together:

2C whole wheat flour
1 tbs. baking powder
1 tsp. cinnamon

In a bowl, beat:

3 tbs. egg replacer mixed with 1/3C water
1C soy milk unflavored
1/3C honey
3 tbs. applesauce

Add dry ingredients, and stir just enough to combine.

Quickly stir in:

1C coarsely grated zucchini
1/2C raisins

Spoon batter into prepared muffin cups, and bake for 25 minutes at 375°. Allow to cool slightly before trying to remove them from the tin.

# WHOLE WHEAT BREAD

*Makes 2 loaves.*

In a small bowl, mix:

1/2 c warm (not hot!) water
1 package of dried yeast
1 tsp maple syrup or honey

Stir gently, then cover and place in warm area (such as the inside of an unlighted gas oven).

In another bowl, combine:

1/3 c water
1 tbsp soy oil
1 tbsp soy sauce

In a large bowl, sift together:

2 c white flour
1 1/4 c whole wheat flour

Add to the flour bowl:

*Continues...*

1/4 c sunflower seeds
4 tbsp bran
3 tbsp oats
2 tbsp red wheat flakes (from health food store)

Make a well in the center of the dry ingredients, and add the wet ingredients – including the yeast mixture. Mix until all is combined. Knead for 15 minutes, turning the dough towards the center. Place the dough in a greased bowl. Cover and let stand in a warm place for 1 hour. (An unlighted gas oven is good for this step as well.)

Remove the dough, which will be doubled in size. Punch it down and knead on a floured board for 15 minutes more.

Divide the bread dough into 2 loaves, mold them into shape and place them on a greased baking sheet. Cover and let stand for 1 hour.

Bake at 375° for 40 to 45 minutes, until the bread sounds hollow when tapped on the bottom.

Allow the loaves to cool before slicing.

# DESSERTS

# CHOCOLATE OR CAROB SLUSH PARFAIT

1C soy milk
1 tsp. vanilla
1 banana
1/2C Rice Cream® with chocolate or carob
   (found in health food stores)
1C ice cubes

Combine in a blender at high speed. Pour mixture into ice cube tray, and freeze for 2 - 3 hours. Put the cubes back in the blender before serving, and make a chocolate or carob ice. Pour out into dessert dishes.

# FROZEN JUICE ON A STICK

Purchase molds at the store to make this treat which is similar to a Popsicle®. Fill the mold with 1/2 fruit juice and 1/2 water. For variety, add diced fresh fruit.

Try berries, peaches, or pineapple.

Fruit smoothies (see page 28) can also be poured into the molds and served frozen.

# BANANAS WITH FRUIT SAUCE

1 c fresh strawberries or 1/2 c raspberries
1 tbsp soy milk
1/2 tsp vanilla
2 bananas, sliced

Purée the first three ingredients in the blender or food processor the first 3 ingredients. Arrange the banana slices in a circle and pour the puree over them. Top with a mint leaf.

# BAKED ORANGE SLICES

In a saucepan, mix:

1/2 c orange juice
1/2 c apple juice
2 tbsp honey
1/4 c raisins
dash of cinnamon
dash of nutmeg

Let simmer until honey is melted (about 3 minutes). Set aside. Peel 2 or 3 oranges, and slice them into quarters. Place orange slices in a small baking dish, and pour sauce over them.

Broil for 6 to 8 minutes. Watch closely! You don't want the slices to burn, but the sauce should thicken slightly.

Serve hot.

# PURÉES

It's simple to purée fruit and freeze it for winter days when there are no local fresh organic berries at your market.

Always buy seasonal fruits. Buy organic whenever possible.

1C fresh berries
1-2 tbs. honey
dash cinnamon

Combine in a blender or food processor until smooth.

When serving right away, try adding fresh fruit like apples or bananas. It enhances the flavor and makes a tasty topping for pancakes or toast. It can also be used as a cereal sweetener and is delicious eaten alone.

You can also freeze the purée in molds inserting stick handles or use the purées with one of the dessert crepes.

Rice milk is a good non-dairy liquid found in health food stores which can be blended right into the purée as a sweetener. Taste it and use whatever amount suits you.

# GELLED FRUIT

This dessert is similar to a fruit salad. It uses Agar. Agar as a thickening agent, which comes from seaweed.

Agar is packaged in different strengths. Read the directions before preparing it in case it differs from mine.

2C cold water
4 tbs. Agar Agar
2C fresh strawberries
1/4C blueberries
1/4C diced apples
3 tbs. lemon juice
2C orange juice
1/4C apple juice
1/4C cherry juice (from fruit drinks)
1/2C pineapple cut into chunks

In a saucepan off the stove, combine 2C cold water with Agar and stir. Let it sit for a few minutes and then add 2C hot water. Now boil for 2 - 3 minutes. In a bowl, combine fresh fruit with lemon juice and toss well. In a separate bowl combine orange, apple, and cherry juice. Mix juice gently with Agar.

Pour into a mold or cake pan, and add the fruit. Stir gently. Chill for at least the whole day.

You can cut this dessert into cubes. Serve it with slices of bananas or papaya.

## GREEN GELLED FRUIT

Follow the directions for Gelled Fruit, and then prepare the following:

1/2C chopped celery
2C chopped pineapple
1/2C pineapple juice
1C orange juice
1C cut kiwi fruit, thin slices
2 tbs. lemon juice
1 tbs. lime juice

Combine fruit and liquids with Agar, and pour into a  mold.

Arranging the kiwi fruit decoratively will make for a beautiful presentation.

# TROPICAL GELLED FRUIT

Follow Agar dissolving directions as in Gelled
Fruit recipe, and then prepare the following:

2C tropical fruits
  (mangos, papayas, pineapples, or bananas)
1C sliced strawberries
1/2C strawberry purée
2C orange juice
1/2C pineapple juice
1 tbs. each lemon and lime juice

Combine fruit, juices and Agar and then pour
into a  mold.  Chill all day.

## AGAR CUSTARD

1/2 lb. tofu
6 tbs. honey
1 tbs. vanilla
3 drops of almond extract
3C purified water
juice from a half of lemon
2 tbs. soy milk
4 tbs. agar flakes
1C water

    Blend (in a food processor) until smooth. Add the soy milk.

    Combine the Agar and water. Stir until dissolved.

    Pour Agar liquid into custard.

    Pour into molds, dessert cups, or a large bowl. Chill.

*Continues...*

## *VARIATIONS:*

**CHOCOLATE OR CAROB CUSTARD -**
*Eliminate the almond extract and substitute 1/4C carob or chocolate powder. Add 2 more tbs. honey, if needed.*

**STRAWBERRY CUSTARD** - *eliminate the almond extract and add 1C strawberry purée. Top with fresh berries.*

**BANANA CUSTARD** - *Eliminate the almond extract and add 1 1/2C fresh banana slices and a dash of vanilla. Top with shredded coconut.*

**ORANGE CUSTARD** - *Eliminate the almond extract and add 1C orange juice and only 2 cups of purified water. Fresh orange slices or mandarin oranges make a great topping.*

# FRUIT COBBLER

Preheat oven to 350°.

6 washed, sliced peaches or pears (with skins)
1/3 c unbleached flour
1 tsp. cinnamon
dash of nutmeg
1/2 c orange juice
1/3 c honey
2 tbsp arrowroot dissolved in 1/4 c cold water

Combine the first four ingredients in a bowl and toss together. Pour into a baking dish. In a saucepan, combine the last three ingredients and heat until the honey is dissolved.

Pour over the fruit. Bake uncovered for 35 minutes at 350°.

Top with chopped nuts or no oil granola. Serve warm.

# BAKED APPLES WITH STRAWBERRIES

4 organically-grown Granny Smith or Macintosh apples

Core the apples and place them standing up in a Pyrex® dish.

1 c water
2 tbsp honey
1/2 tsp cinnamon
sprinkle of ground cloves

In a saucepan, heat and combine the ingredients. Pour the mixture over the apples. Bake at 350° for 35 minutes.

Remove and cool slightly. Serve with sliced strawberries and some of the liquid poured over the apples. Top with chopped nuts.

## RICE PUDDING

Prepare brown rice to yield 2 1/2 cups cooked.
(See grain chart on page 15.)

2 1/2 c soy milk
2 tbsp honey
2 tbsp molasses
1 tsp vanilla
2 tbsp agar-agar flakes
(a natural gelling agent that comes from seaweed
and is found in health food stores)

Combine all ingredients except rice in a
saucepan and bring to a boil stirring. Turn down heat,
and simmer until thick (just a few minutes)
Then add:

1 tsp orange juice
1/2 c dates or raisins

In a baking dish, spread out the cooked rice and
pour the soy milk mixture over it. Bake at 350° for
about an hour.
You may top this with no-oil cookie crumbs.
Great served hot or cold!

# CASHEW RICE PUDDING

1 pint amasaki
(a rice syrup found in health food stores)
3 1/2 tbs. kuzu (arrowroot)
1/4C water
1/2 tsp. vanilla
2 tbs. cashew butter
(optional, but this adds a wonderful taste)

Heat amasaki to scalding. Dissolve the arrowroot in water, adding it slowly and whisking quickly so as not to get lumps. Add the vanilla and cashew butter, and combine well.

Pour into a dish or dessert molds, and chill. Serve with chopped nuts.

## CAROB CREAM PIE

Prepare a 9" pie crust by crumbling 6 oz.
Honey Grahams® Crackers with a dash of olive oil.
Spread this evenly onto a non-stick pie tin. Bake at
350° for 15 minutes and then chill for 1 hour.

1 lbs. tofu
1/2C soy milk
1 capful vanilla
3/4C honey
1 tbs. canola oil
3/4C carob powder

Blend all of the ingredients in a food processor
until smooth. Taste for sweetness. Adding 1 tbs. of
molasses adds a nice flavor. Pour the custard into the
chilled pie crust, and refrigerate for a few hours. Nuts
and banana slices are a good topping for this pie.

## TOFU CHEESECAKE

Prepare a 9" pie crust by crumbling 6 oz. Honey Graham® Crackers with a dash of olive oil. Spread this evenly onto a non-stick pie tin. Bake at 350° for 15 minutes and then chill.

2 lbs. of tofu
1 tbs. canola oil
1/4C soy milk
1 tsp. vanilla
1/3C lemon juice
dash of salt (optional)

Blend all of the ingredients in a food processor until smooth. Pour into prepared pie crust, and bake at 350° for 45 minutes. Cool for 1 hour then chill in the refrigerator.

Serve with fresh fruit purée and fresh fruit.

# FRUITY COUSCOUS CAKE

2C mixed fruit or berries
5C apple juice
3 tbs. lemon juice
1 tbs. grated lemon rind
2C coucous

Bring apple juice and lemon juice to a boil. Slowly add the rind and couscous, and stir until thick. Pour into a cake pan, and combine the fresh fruit. Allow to cool and then chill for 2 hours.

Toasted nuts and fruit puree taste great when this cake is sliced and served.

# STRAWBERRY TOFU CREAM

1/2 lb. firm tofu
2 tbs. honey
1C sliced, washed strawberries
2 tbs. maple syrup
dash of vanilla
dash of nutmeg
dash of cinnamon
1 tbs. lemon juice

Purée in a food processor until smooth. You may need to add a little water to get the creamy consistency. This will keep for a few days in the refrigerator; and if it separates, just whip it up again.

Any fruit can be added in place of or in addition to the strawberries.

This is also wonderful for breakfast.

# SOY WHIPPED CREAM

Blend the following ingredients together and then chill:

1 1/2 lbs. tofu
2 - 4 tbs. canola oil
6 tbs. honey
1/4C soy milk with vanilla
juice from 1 lemon

## TOFU PUMPKIN PIE

2 - 1 lb. cakes of firm tofu
1/3C brown rice syrup
1 tbs. barley malt syrup
1 tbs. maple syrup
16 oz. can pumpkin purée
2 tsp. cinnamon
1/2 tsp. allspice
1/2 tsp. nutmeg
1/2 tsp. ginger

Blend the first four ingredients until creamy. Pour into a bowl, and add the pumpkin purée and the spices. Stir until all of the ingredients are combined. Pour into a pre-baked pie shell (see tofu cheesecake on page 272), and bake for 15 minutes at 425°. Chill until you are ready to serve it. Top with chopped nuts.

# TOFU BANANA PARFAIT

*Serves 4.*

4 oz. soft tofu
1 small ripe banana
1/3C apple juice
3 tbs. fruit purée or concentrate
1/2C berries
1 large very ripe peach (or papaya)
1 kiwi, peeled and sliced into thin rounds
4 mint leaves

Combine and purée in a blender the first four ingredients. Freeze in an ice cube tray for 30 minutes, and return to blender. Purée until light and creamy.

In parfait glasses, first add 1 tbs. of berries and then some peach slices.

Arrange 2 kiwi slices along the outside of the parfait glass.

Pour the purée 1/2 way up. Finish adding the berries and peaches, and fill to the top with the banana purée. Top with a kiwi slice and mint leaf. You can change fruits to seasonal availability.

## BOOKS

**GOOD FOOD TODAY, GREAT KIDS TOMORROW.**
by **Jay Gordon, M. D.** with **Antonia Barnes Boyle.**
The easy-to-read, practical book for parents which answers the most often-asked questions about making correct food choices for happy, healthy children: Pediatrician/nutritionist Gordon clearly explains the power of diet for a child's health and well being. *232 pages.*

### GREAT FOOD FOR GREAT KIDS RECIPES:

*Quick and Easy Recipes for a Healthy Family.*
By **Meyera Robbins** whose healthy and delicious meals were an instant *hit* in her Los Angeles restaurant. With new and exciting meals springing from her kitchen at home, Meyera is a *hit* with her daughter Simone and her husband Jay Gordon on a daily basis. Learn how to cook healthy kid-tested foods that taste great! Over **200 easy-to-follow recipes** that make preparing and eating healthy meals a wonderful experience for the whole family. Learn how to shop for healthy foods, and create delicious meals with no sugar, fat, or salt. *300 pages.*

### HOW THE NEW FOOD LABELS CAN SAVE YOUR LIFE!

By **Peg Jordan, R. N.**, journalist, and consumer health advocate.This eye-opening book presents fresh insights on how to read the new food labels to make healthy food choices, prevent chronic, life-threatening diseases and achieve optimum health. *144 pages.*

## AUDIOTAPES

**GOOD FOOD TODAY, GREAT KIDS TOMORROW:** In this insightful six-volume audio set, Dr. Jay Gordon answers the most often-asked questions about making correct food choices for healthy, happy children. Covering birth to adolescence, you'll learn how to set healthy eating patterns today that will lead your children to a lifetime of smart choices. The tapes cover how to handle school lunches, the challenges of special times such as parties, holidays, and vacations, the problems of obesity and eating disorders, and a host of other timely topics that concern every parent. *6 audiotapes.*

## VIDEOS

**GOOD FOOD TODAY, GREAT KIDS TOMORROW:** Join Dr. Jay Gordon and other parents in a lively round table discussion that will improve the way you and your family eat – forever! This video covers tough subjects such as junk food cravings, healthy meals and snacks, school lunches, self-esteem, peer pressure, and much more. *Approx. One Hour.*

**JAY GORDON TALKS TO KIDS ABOUT FOOD:** Entertaining one-on-one talks with some of America's most health conscious kids. Contains information for all children's age groups. Learn new and exciting ways to help your children begin eating right – today! You'll be giving your kids the gift of good health! Dr. Jay Gordon's unique approach will teach you how to motivate your children to develop healthy eating habits that will last a lifetime. Watch this program with your whole family! It's packed with ideas that ensure better health. *Approx. One Hour.*

## O  R  D  E  R       F  O  R  M

**Send To: Michael Wiese Productions**
   **4354 Laurel Canyon Blvd., Suite 234, Studio City, CA 91604**

*Please send me the following:*

| Quantity | | Price | Sub-total |
|---|---|---|---|
| | **THE COMPLETE SET (Regular Price $125.70, SAVE $15.75!!)** | **$109.95** | _____ |
| | *You receive all the following six items.* | | |

*Or you may order each item individually:*

| | | | |
|---|---|---|---|
| _____ | GOOD FOOD TODAY, GREAT KIDS TOMORROW *book* | **$17.95** | _____ |
| _____ | GOOD FOOD FOR GREAT KIDS RECIPES *book* | 17.95 | _____ |
| _____ | HOW THE NEW FOOD LABELS CAN SAVE YOUR LIFE *book* | 9.95 | _____ |
| _____ | GOOD FOOD TODAY, GREAT KIDS TOMORROW *audio set (6)* | 39.95 | _____ |
| _____ | GOOD FOOD TODAY, GREAT KIDS TOMORROW *video #1* | 19.95 | _____ |
| _____ | JAY TALKS TO *KIDS* ABOUT FOOD *video #2* | 19.95 | _____ |
| | | Sub-total | _____ |

| **Shipping & Handling** | **SHIPPING/HANDLING** (see left) | _____ |
|---|---|---|
| $4 per item or $12 for the complete set. | CA Residents add 8.25% **SALES TAX** | _____ |
| | **TOTAL ENCLOSED $** | _____ |

*Please make check payable to Michael Wiese Productions.  Please allow 3 - 4 weeks for delivery.*

**CREDIT CARD ORDERS CALL**
**1-800-379-8808**

❑ **Master Card**   ❑ **Visa**

Credit Card Number:
_____ • _____ • _____ • _____

Expir. Date:_____

Cardholder Name:

Cardholder Signature:

NAME: _____

ADDRESS: _____

_____

CITY: _____

STATE: _____ ZIP _____

TELEPHONE: _____